Wales Wood

A history of the Ninety-fifth regiment, Illinois infantry volunteers : from its organization in the fall of 1862, until its final discharge from the United States service, in 1865

Wales Wood

A history of the Ninety-fifth regiment, Illinois infantry volunteers : from its organization in the fall of 1862, until its final discharge from the United States service, in 1865

ISBN/EAN: 9783337185084

Printed in Europe, USA, Canada, Australia, Japan

Cover: Foto ©ninafisch / pixelio.de

More available books at **www.hansebooks.com**

A

HISTORY

OF THE

NINETY-FIFTH REGIMENT

ILLINOIS INFANTRY VOLUNTEERS,

FROM ITS ORGANIZATION IN THE FALL OF 1862, UNTIL ITS FINAL
DISCHARGE FROM THE UNITED STATES SERVICE, IN 1865.

By WALES W. WOOD, Esq.,
(Former Adjutant of Regiment.)

CHICAGO:
TRIBUNE COMPANY'S BOOK AND JOB PRINTING OFFICE.
1865.

Entered according to Act of Congress in the year 1865, by

WALES W. WOOD,

In the Clerk's Office of the District Court of the United States, for the Northern District of Illinois.

J. L. BATCHELDER, BINDER,
McCormick's Block, S. E. cor. Randolph & Dearborn.

TO THE

COMMISSIONED OFFICERS AND ENLISTED MEN

OF THE

NINETY-FIFTH REGIMENT

ILLINOIS INFANTRY VOLUNTEERS,

This volume is respectfully dedicated, by

THE AUTHOR.

PREFACE.

DURING the past summer, while the 16th Army Corps lay in camp at Montgomery, Alabama, the author commenced writing a historical report of the Ninety-fifth Illinois Infantry, from its organization, with the view merely of having the same entered upon the regimental books, and become a part of the regimental records, for future reference and information.

The commissioned officers and enlisted men having urgently requested its publication, that each member of the command and others interested might be supplied with a copy, it has been deemed advisable to issue the history in the form of the present volume.

In submitting the work to the public, the author is aware that it contains nothing of particular interest to any, except the survivors of the regiment, the friends of its deceased members, and the people of the counties in which it was raised; and it is more especially for their benefit that the present publication appears.

It is believed, however, that works of this nature will prove of great assistance to the general historian, in writing up his record of the Rebellion. If each regiment present its history from the beginning, prepared accurately by one of its own members, the general writer may then be able to cull therefrom much of the material necessary to a complete and reliable history of the late war against the Union.

The author is indebted to Lieut. Amos J. Boyington, of Company "A," Corporal Robert Horan and Private Samuel Pepper, of Company "G," for the use of their diaries kept on the Red River, Guntown and Arkansas expeditions, and also to other officers and enlisted men of the regiment, for valuable information from time to time imparted.

CHICAGO, ILL., Nov. 15, 1865.

CONTENTS.

CHAPTER I.

Organization of Regiment at Camp Fuller — Drills and Parades — Discipline — Military abatement of a Whisky Shop — Orders to proceed to Louisville, Ky., countermanded — Incidents on return of Regiment to Camp Fuller — Regiment afterward ordered to Columbus, Ky..13—25

CHAPTER II.

Journey of the Regiment to Cairo, Ill., and Columbus, Ky. — Report to General Davis, at Columbus — The Iron Cable — The trip to Jackson, Tenn. — Camp Life at Jackson — How a Ninety-fifth Man supposed himself captured by a Rebel Cavalryman, and how he was mistaken — Ordered to Grand Junction, Tenn. — Report to Brig. General Hamilton — Assigned to General McArthur's Division, 13th Army Corps — Incidents of Camp Life at Grand Junction — Preparations for a forward movement........26—38

CHAPTER III.

The Movement from Grand Junction — A tedious Day's March — Fatigue of the Men — Iron Accessions to Knapsacks — Crossing the Tallahatchie — Halt at Abbeville — Advance to Yockena — News of Van Dorn's Raid into Holly Springs — Return of the Army — Expedition to Salem, Miss. — Anecdote of a Jug — March of the Regiment to Memphis...................39—52

viii   CONTENTS.

CHAPTER IV.

Expedition from Memphis down the River against Vicksburg — Arrival at.Milliken's Bend — The Canal near Young's Point — Colonel Deitzler's Brigade ordered to Lake Providence — Important order affecting the Ninety-fifth — The Canal at Lake Providence — Sickness and Death in the Regiment — Raising of Colored Regiments — Policy of the Government concerning Slavery during the Rebellion, reviewed — Resignation of Colonel Church — March of the Army from Milliken's Bend to "Hard Times" Landing — Ninety-fifth transferred to General Ransom's Brigade — Crossing to Grand Gulf — March to rear of Vicksburg — Charges of 19th and 22nd of May — The Siege — Surrender of the City — General Ransom's Brigade sent to Natchez — Its operations while there — Its return to Vicksburg...................53—91

CHAPTER V.

Expeditions from Vicksburg in Spring of 1864 — Sherman's March to Meridian — Colonel Coates' defense of Yazoo City — The Red River Expedition — Taking of Fort DeRussey — Ninety-fifth detailed to destroy the works — Arrival at Alexandria — March to Grand Ecore — Ascending the River on Transports — Battle of Pleasant Hill — Retreat ordered by General Banks — Return of the Fleet — Running Batteries at Vandares — Ninety-fifth as Rear Guard of Banks' Army — Two Days' Fight at Clouterville — Retreat to Alexandria — Battle of Yellow Bayou — Evacuation of the Red River Country — Return of the Ninety-fifth to Vicksburg..92—108

CHAPTER VI.

Arrival of the Regiment at Memphis — Assigned to General Sturgis' Expedition — March from Memphis — Battle of Guntown, Miss. — Colonel Humphrey killed — Captain Stewart takes command, and is severely wounded — Death of Captain Bush — Command taken by Captain Schellenger — The Regiment fight with desperation — Ammunition giving out — Absence of Commanding Officers — Ninety-fifth fall back, after a long conflict against superior odds — Form second line of battle — Final Retreat on Memphis — Hardships — Arrival of the Regiment back to Memphis in deplorable condition — Comments on the Guntown affair..109—116

CHAPTER VII.

The Regiment relieved from duty for a time after the Guntown Battle, and allowed to recruit — The Command soon regains a prosperous condition, and prepares for the Arkansas Expedition, under General Mower — Arrival at St. Charles, Ark. — Company "K" detached and left at the mouth of White River as Garrison — Regiment ascends White River to Duvall's Bluff, and goes by Railroad to Brownsville — The lengthy March through Arkansas to Missouri in search of Price — Arrival at Camp Girardeau — "Colonel Pap," and why he was so named — Regiment embarks for St. Louis, and goes to Jefferson City — Ordered forward to Sedalia — Assigned to Garrison Duty — Remain there until the Campaign against Price closes — General A. J. Smith's troops sent to Benton Barracks, St. Louis....................117—124

CHAPTER VIII.

Operations of Hood in Tennessee — His Advance on Nashville — Battles at Columbia, Spring Hill, and Franklin — General Smith's Command ordered to Reënforce General Thomas at Nashville — Leaves St. Louis on Transports, and proceeds to Cairo — Voyage up the Ohio and Cumberland Rivers — Safe arrival at Nashville — Detachments of the Ninety-fifth rejoin the Regiment — Account of the Georgia Detachment during General Sherman's Campaign — Active preparations made around Nashville to receive Hood — His Army in sight — The Ninety-fifth holds an important Position in the Defenses of the City — Work on the Fortifications — Thomas moves his Army out to attack Hood — Great Battles of December 15th and 16th, 1864 — Hood's Army defeated and driven back in confusion — Part taken by the Ninety-fifth — The Pursuit to the Tennessee River — General Smith's Troops ascend the river and go into Winter Quarters, at Eastport, Miss. — Expedition to Corinth

—The Hard-tack Famine at Eastport—Corn issued to the Troops—The Boys desire to draw Halters—Arrival of Rations—Preparations for another active Campaign—Transports arrive to convey the Troops to New Orleans............125—156

CHAPTER IX.

The Ninety-fifth embarks on the "Adam Jacobs" for New Orleans—Fleet proceeds down the Tennessee River—Arrival at Cairo—Depredations committed there by the Troops—Voyage down the Mississippi—General Smith's forces disembark at Vicksburg—Afterward proceed to New Orleans—Disagreeable Camp below the City on the old Battle-fields—Regiment goes to Dauphine Island by way of Lake Pontchartrain—Arrival at the Island—Expedition of Colonel Moore's Brigade to Cedar Point, and up the west side of the Bay toward Mobile—Oysters and Musquitoes at Cedar Point—Advance up the Country—How the Music was used to deceive the Enemy—The 44th Missouri Band—Return of the Brigade to Cedar Point—Crosses the Bay, and rejoins 16th Army Corps at Dauley's Landing, on Fish River—General Canby's Army advances on Spanish Fort and Blakely—Investment of both Places—The part performed by the Ninety-fifth in the Reduction of Spanish Fort—Both Strongholds taken by Assault—Fall of Mobile........................157—176

CHAPTER X.

The 16th Army Corps ordered to Montgomery, Alabama—Rumors received before leaving Blakely, of General Grant's victories in the East—The suspicion with which the Ninety-fifth received flying reports, since they were deceived at "Big Sandy"—General Grant's success confirmed—Enthusiasm with which the Intelligence was received by the Regiments—The Ninety-fifth cheer lustily—The March through the Pine Forests—Guideboards—A Rattlesnake Affair—Arrival at Greenville—The Ninety-fifth garrison the Town—Feelings of the Inhabitants—A Paper published by the Soldiers—March continued to Montgomery—Arrival there—General Wilson's Raid through this

Section — Tooops camp around the City — Rebel paroled Soldiers from the Eastern Armies pass through — Beauregard, Bragg, Pillow, Semmes — Dick Taylor and Kirby Smith surrender — The Rebellion at an end — Drills resumed by the Ninety-fifth — What General A. J. Smith thought of their Dress Parade — Anecdote of the "Pointer Dog," and how Colonel Blanden came by it — Order from the War Department to Muster out Troops — The Men anxious to get Home — The 16th Corps retained for Garrison Duty in Northern Alabama..............................177—193

CHAPTER XI.

A portion of the 16th Army Corps sent to North-eastern Alabama — Col. Moore's Brigade garrison Tuskegee, Opelika, and Union Springs — The Ninety-fifth occupy Opelika — Feelings of the Citizens — Stringent Whisky Orders enforced by Col. Blanden — Management of the Negro Question — Paroled Rebel Soldiers — The Fourth of July, and how the Soldiers Celebrated it at Opelika — Officers and Men anxious to be Mustered Out — The Regiment relieved, and returns to Montgomery to be sent home — Proceeds to Vicksburg via Selma, Meridian, and Jackson — Arrival at Vicksburg — Takes Steamer up the River to St. Louis — Goes thence to Springfield, Ill., for final Payment and Discharge — Mustered out of the Service at "Camp Butler" — Return home to McHenry and Boone Counties — The Receptions there given the various Companies — Conclusion............194—210

APPENDIX.

Roster of Commissioned Officers and Non-commissioned Staff, showing Muster in, Resignations, Deaths and Promotions during Service..211
List showing Commissioned Officers and Enlisted Men mustered out with Regiment, Transferred, Discharged, Died and Deserted..216
List of Commissioned Officers and Enlisted Men wounded while in Service..232
List of Commissioned Officers and Enlisted Men killed in Action..237
List of Campaigns and Battles in which the Regiment took part..239

Tabular Statement, showing number of Commissioned Officers and Enlisted Men Mustered out, Transferred, Discharged, Died, Deserted, and aggregate Number belonging to the Regiment during Service..240

HISTORY.

CHAPTER I.

Organization of Regiment at Camp Fuller — Drills and Parades — Discipline — Military abatement of a Whisky Shop — Orders to proceed to Louisville, Ky., countermanded — Incidehts on return of Regiment to Camp Fuller — Regiment afterward ordered to Columbus, Ky.

UNDER the call for six hundred thousand more volunteers, made by President Lincoln in the summer of 1862, to aid in putting down the rebellion, the organization of the Ninety-fifth Regiment Illinois Infantry Volunteers was formed, and composed of seven companies from McHenry county, and three companies from Boone.

Enlistments in these companies commenced briskly in both counties, in the latter part of July of that year, and the volunteering progressed with such enthusiasm and rapidity, that on the first of August following several of the companies had obtained the minimum number of recruits required by law, and by the fifteenth of the same month all were filled to near the maximum standard, and were ready to be assigned to regiments, or to be consolidated into one regimental organization. The officers and men of the companies thus raised, coming as they did from neighboring counties, early expressed a desire to go into the United States service as a regiment, and to effect such object a convention was held at Marengo, Illinois, on the 16th day of August, 1862, when the future field, staff and line officers of the command for the first time assembled, became acquainted with each other, and decided upon the military organization. At this meeting the Hon. Daniel Whitney, a citizen and pioneer of Boone county, was called to the chair, who stated the objects of the convention, and addressed the officers who were about going forth to the defense of the country, eloquently and with patriotism. The main business before the meeting was the selection of field officers for the new regiment, and Hon. Lawrence S. Church, of Woodstock, McHenry county, was unanimously chosen as its Colonel; Thomas W. Humphrey, of DeKalb county, Lieutenant Colonel; and Leander Blanden, of Harvard, McHenry county, as Major. The proceedings of the convention were conducted in the best spirit and harmony, and it adjourned with the satisfaction of having given shape and consolidation to the ten companies anxiously awaiting its action.

Soon afterward, Governor Yates accepted the regiment, designated its number, and directed the companies to rendezvous at "Camp Fuller," Rockford, Illinois, for the purpose of completing the regimental organization and muster into the United States service. Accordingly, on the third day of September, 1862, the different companies arrived at the rendezvous indicated, taking quarters in barracks erected by Government for the new troops. On the fourth day of the same month the regiment was mustered into the service of the United States by Lieut. J. W. Tibbatts, of the regular army, and at that time the Roster of Commissioned Officers thus mustered was as follows:

FIELD AND STAFF.

COLONEL	LAWRENCE S. CHURCH.
LIEUT. COLONEL	THOMAS W. HUMPHREY.
MAJOR	LEANDER BLANDEN.
ADJUTANT	WALES W. WOOD.
SURGEON	GEORGE N. WOODWARD.
ASST. SURGEON	WALTER F. SUITER.
" "	A. D. MERRITT.
QUARTERMASTER	HENRY D. BATES.
CHAPLAIN	THOS. R. SATTERFIELD.

COMPANY "A."

CAPTAIN	WILLIAM AVERY.
1ST LIEUTENANT	ALEXANDER S. STEWART.
2ND LIEUTENANT	JAMES E. SPONABLE.

COMPANY "B."

CAPTAIN	CHARLES B. LOOP.
1ST LIEUTENANT	MILTON E. KEELER.
2ND LIEUTENANT	AARON F. RANDALL.

COMPANY "C."

CAPTAIN	JASON B. MANZER.
1ST LIEUTENANT	WM. W. WEDGEWOOD.
2ND LIEUTENANT	OTIS H. SMITH.

COMPANY "D."

CAPTAIN	EDWARD J. COOK.
1ST LIEUTENANT	JOHN E. BECKLEY.
2ND LIEUTENANT	WM. H. HUFFMAN.

COMPANY "E."

CAPTAIN	JOHN EDDY.
1ST LIEUTENANT	ASA FARNUM.
2ND LIEUTENANT	OSCAR E. DOWE.

COMPANY "F."

CAPTAIN	WM. H. STEWART,
1ST LIEUTENANT	SABINE VAN CUREN.
2ND LIEUTENANT	PHINEAS H. KERR.

COMPANY "G."

CAPTAIN	ELLIOTT N. BUSH.
1ST LIEUTENANT	HENRY M. BUSH.
2ND LIEUTENANT	JOSEPH M. COLLYER.

COMPANY "H."

CAPTAIN	CHARLES H. TRYON.
1ST LIEUTENANT	JAMES H. WETMORE.
2ND LIEUTENANT	WM. B. WALKER.

COMPANY "I."

CAPTAIN.....................JAMES NISH.
1ST LIEUTENANT ....GARDNER S. SOUTHWORTH.
2ND LIEUTENANT..............CONVERSE PIERCE.

COMPANY "K."

CAPTAIN.....................GABRIEL E. CORNWELL.
1ST LIEUTENANT..............ALMON SCHELLENGER.
2ND LIEUTENANT..............ALONZO BROOKS.

On the same day, September 4th, 1862, the Colonel commanding the regiment, by Regimental Order No. one, made appointments of non-commissioned officers for the several companies, and on the 9th, the non-commissioned staff was ordered as follows:

SERGEANT MAJOR..................BENNETT T. WAKEMAN.
QUARTERMASTER SERGEANT..........WM. H. EARLEY.
COMMISSARY SERGEANT.............JOHN B. HURLBUT.
HOSPITAL STEWARD................WILBUR P. BUCK.
DRUM MAJOR......................JUSTUS M. SHEFFIELD.
FIFE MAJOR ....THEODORE INGHAM.

Soon after the muster in and completion of the regimental organization, the regiment began inquiring studiously into the "Revised Army Regulations" and "Tactics," and preparing for the real and active service before them in the field. It was known that the regiment would remain at Camp Fuller a few weeks before leaving the State, and meanwhile the commissioned officers and enlisted men, heretofore unaccustomed to the conditions of military life, had a good opportunity of becoming acquainted with some of its mysteries and requirements, of studying into the theoretical part of war, and of informing themselves generally in reference to the duties appertaining to their respective offices. Squad drills, company and battalion drills, dress parades, and commissioned and non-commissioned officers' schools at night, were at once instituted, and the whole camp, from morning till evening, now became busy with the hum and tramp of military preparation.

During the same fall, three other regiments—the Seventy-fourth, Ninety-second, and Ninety-sixth Illinois Infantry—raised in Northern Illinois, were in rendezvous camp at Rockford at the same time with the Ninety-fifth, and among them all arose a friendly intercourse of brothers in arms. A spirit of rivalry sprang up, commendable to the officers and soldiers of the different organizations, and beneficial to the service they were about entering upon.

After the departure of the Seventy-fourth Illinois for the field, Colonel Church, being senior in rank, was placed in command of the Post, and while administering in this capacity, won the praise of all, and gave entire satisfaction to the other regiments, as well as his own. Most of the time, however, during the encampment at Camp Fuller, Colonel Church's health was very feeble. The sick bed seemed a much more appropriate place for him than the camp, yet his ardent patriotism, and an overruling desire to be with his men all the time, determined him to remain with them, though already prostrated with sickness. The duties of commanding and disciplining the regiment therefore devolved much of the time upon Lieut. Col. Humphrey, who exerted himself energetically and constantly to promote the welfare and efficiency of the command, and give it as thorough preparation as possible for the field. Under his rigid but beneficial discipline, and assisted by instructions from Lieut. Sellers, of the 36th Illinois Infantry, who was employed as drill-master, the regiment made rapid progress, and in a few weeks could perform dress-parade, guard-mounting, and the various maneuvres and evolutions prescribed in the Tactics, with much credit and a good degree of proficiency, as was judged by those who had seen active military service.

The regiment at this encampment was within a few hours ride of home, and day after day, during their stay there, the friends and acquaintances of the soldiers came flocking in from all parts of Boone and McHenry counties, attracted thither by the great interest taken in the welfare of the regiment, and bringing with them large and benevolent supplies of eatables and luxuries palatable to the taste, and conducive to the comfort and contentment of the "boys in blue." To such an extent was the generosity of the good and loyal people of those counties carried in this respect, that provisions of all kinds — not known in the commissary department of the army — appeared in great abundance and superfluity upon the mess tables of commissioned officers and private soldiers alike. Amid such liberal niceties of the season the ordinary rations of "hard tack,"— coffee, sugar, meat, and-so-forth,— provided for the soldier by the Government, were somewhat at discount, and his appetite did not crave while these profuse gifts were continually pouring in from the hands of a generous and warm-hearted public. It might be thought, as a sanitary consideration, that the light and sweetened food thus freely furnished to the inmates of the camp would not fit them properly for the hard knocks of military life, and since sooner or later they were to come to it, that hard-cracker without butter, coffee without milk, potatoes desiccated, and pork and beans, were the substantials on which soldiers should be prepared for the field. The boys of the Ninety-fifth, however, did not thus consider the matter, and during their sojourn at Camp Fuller, the varieties of eatables sent in to overflowing failed not to find in them thankful and happy recipients and greedy consumers.

Notwithstanding the excitement consequent upon the arrival in camp, daily, of such multitudes of visitors, the drills, parades and disciplining of the regiment progressed in a favorable and highly satisfactory manner.

The orders, while here, were quite strict, not allowing officers or enlisted men to visit their homes, except in few instances, and then only on proper authority. Some of the men, not then fully comprehending the necessity of that severe discipline which thus early in the service bound them down to strict regulations, and desirous of enjoying home associations as much as possible before taking final leave for the war, carried into effect their mischievous inclinations, and, unbeknown to the Colonel commanding, took the benefit of what is termed in the army "French furlough." Such did not stand upon the order of their going, but went without orders. Only a few cases of this kind occurred, however, and the general conduct of the command while at Rockford was good and soldierly throughout.

While in camp at this point, a certain Irishman located and opened an establishment, in close proximity to the regimental camp, for the purpose of retailing intoxicating beverages to soldiers. This matter was brought to the notice of the Lt. Colonel commanding rather strikingly one day, as certain parties were observed to be returning from that locality, not walking in the strictest line possible, nor seemingly over ground of the most level character. Other indications were manifested in their bearing going plainly to show that these few men of the Ninety-fifth had imbibed somewhat in excess of moderation at the Irishman's shop, and that they were not living strictly up to the temperance pledge, if indeed they ever took it. Colonel Humphrey therefore notified the proprietor of the alcoholic establishment that his trade in spirituous liquors so near to the camp was having a deleterious effect upon the command, producing conduct prejudicial to good order and military discipline, and warned him to move his whisky concern from that vicinity immediately.

The proprietor thereof, however, supposing the United States of America to be a free country, where every one could do as he pleased, and not being accustomed to the practical promulgation and enforcement of military orders, could not see the matter in the same light in which the Lt. Colonel viewed it, and concluded to keep open his doors and continue the practice of dealing out strong drinks to whoever thirsted in that locality, without reference to the military commander and in disregard of his opinions or orders on the subject. Colonel Humphrey now determined that the nuisance should be at once abated by military force, and that the evil which could not be suppressed by persuasion, should be eradicated and banished by means of coercion. He accordingly ordered a detachment of his command, in charge of a commissioned officer, to proceed to the liquor shop, arrest the proprietor, seize the whisky, load the same into a wagon provided for the purpose, and report to regimental head-quarters without delay. The party detailed, promptly obeyed and literally carried into effect the order for arrest and confiscation. The whisky dealer was brought in, surrounded with bristling bayonets, and the vinous contents of the alcoholic institution were soon safely deposited at regimental head-quarters, and stowed away for safe keeping, to await further action and orders. The result of the whole matter was, that the keeper of the shop, being released, went to the city of Rockford and made complaint to the civil authorities of his grievances. A certain judge afterward came to regimental head-quarters and arranged with the commanding officer as follows: that the owner of the property confiscated be allowed to resume possession thereof, but that he remove both himself and his rummery away from the vicinity of that encampment forthwith.

On the 29th day of September, 1862, orders were received from Governor Yates for the regiment to leave the State immediately, after receiving pay and bounty, proceed to Louisville, Kentucky, and report for duty to Major General H. G. Wright, commanding the Department of the Ohio. The camp was astir early on the morning of the day set for departing from Camp Fuller, and the soldiers, little supposing that they were to return thither so soon as they afterward did, made bonfires of almost everything combustible about camp in the shape of old barrels, boxes, mess-tables and benches. The barracks were left standing, but certain compartments of those even had been rendered so unpleasant, that, to say the least, their condition would not be of an inviting character to returning occupants, and would require some police duty before their use could be again tolerated. At an early hour of the same day, the regiment took up its line of march through the city of Rockford to the railroad depot, and filled the cars provided for conveying the command to Chicago. Scarcely, however, was the embarkation finished when Colonel Church received a telegram from Governor Yates which rescinded the former order of march, and directed him to return to Camp

Fuller with his command and remain there until further orders. In compliance, the regiment marched back to the old camp — all tired and disappointed in not getting off for the war.

And now the men began to wish they possessed the benches and mess-tables, and various articles of military household furniture, which a short time previous they had consigned to the flames, under supposition that such conveniences would never be again needed. Certain ones well remembered, too, in what plight their quarters at the barracks had been left, and the mischievous circumstance which had furnished the boys with much fun and merriment at the outset, was now, in a practical application to themselves, not so much of a laughing matter after all.

The regiment now resumed drilling, and employed the time usefully until October 30th, when new orders were received from Adjutant General Fuller, at Springfield, to move the command immediately to Columbus, Kentucky, and report for duty to Major General U. S. Grant, commanding the Department and Army of the Tennessee.

CHAPTER II.

Journey of the Regiment to Cairo, Ill., and Columbus, Ky.— Report to General Davis, at Columbus — The Iron Cable — The trip to Jackson, Tenn. — Camp Life at Jackson — How a Ninety-fifth Man supposed himself captured by a Rebel Cavalryman, and how he was mistaken — Ordered to Grand Junction, Tenn. — Report to Brig. General Hamilton — Assigned to General McArthur's Division, 13th Army Corps — Incidents of Camp Life at Grand Junction — Preparations for a forward movement.

ON the fourth day of November, 1862, in accordance with orders from head-quarters of the State, the regiment took the cars at Rockford, passing over the North-Western road to Chicago, and proceeded thence to Cairo, Ill., by the Illinois Central. At the time of leaving "Camp Fuller" for the seat of war, it numbered as follows:

Commissioned Officers.................. 39
Enlisted Men...........................944

Aggregate 983

most of whom accompanied the regiment, and only a very few sick soldiers were left behind. The command arrived at Cairo on the morning of November 6th, after a long and tedious ride over the Illinois Central Railroad, and immediately embarked on the steamer "Dacotah" for Columbus, Ky.; landed at that place in the afternoon of the same day, and reported for orders to Brigadier General Davis, commanding the district. He instructed the Colonel to keep his regiment on the boat until evening, when railroad transportation would be furnished to Jackson, Tenn. It was here that Colonel L. S. Church, who, though in feeble health, had attended the regiment hither, having been wearied and broken down still more by the long journey, was obliged to leave the command and return to his home. He did this with much reluctance on his part, and to the deep regret of the entire regiment, but under the most urgent advice and solicitation of medical officers. All saw that his health was rapidly failing, that his speedy return North was necessary for his recovery; and it was with many a sorrowful feeling that his officers and men bade him farewell, still hoping, however, that, with health restored, he would come again to command them and take part in those busy military scenes upon which the regiment was now entering.

At Columbus the curiosity of all was excited at the sight of the bluffy stronghold which a few months previous had been in rebel possession, and which for some time served as a formidable barrier to Federal navigation of the Mississippi river. The important military movements from Cairo and other points in the spring of '62 had necessitated its evacuation. While occupying the place, the rebels had sunk a huge iron chain or cable in the river above the town, fastened to either shore, to prevent the downward passage of Union boats, and a portion of it could still be seen hanging in broken condition over the bluffs, showing exactly the location of the obstruction in the times of its usefulness to the Confederacy. At the wharf another piece of this chain, which had been fished out of the river, was lying coiled up, and attracted crowds of the men, who were curious to examine the monster cable about which so much had been said and written. The desire to collect relics of the war already manifested itself, and one soldier expressed an ardent wish to secure a portion of the chain and preserve the same as a curiosity. It was wisely concluded, however, that the men had quite enough traps on hand already, quite enough baggage and sufficiently full knapsacks without being encumbered by such ponderous material as superfluous iron.

Toward evening of the same day, November 6th, orders came for the regiment to debark from the steamer and proceed by railroad to Jackson, Tennessee, reporting there to Major General S. A. Hurlbut, commanding that district. The cars provided for the trip were filled to overflowing, the loading was finished during the evening, and at a late hour the train moved out for its destination. Freight cars were employed on this road for transporting troops, and it was the first time in the lives of the passengers that they had had the pleasure of an excursion in that particular kind of vehicles. Yet there was no murmuring on this account among the soldiers, for they were traveling upon a military railroad, from which rebels had run off or destroyed a great share of the rolling stock, and they cheerfully accepted such regulations and accommodations as the circumstances of war afforded. The regiment arrived safely at Jackson at about one o'clock on the morning of November 7th, and was immediately reported to Major General Hurlbut as ordered. He directed Lt. Col. Humphrey to keep his command upon or near the cars until morning, when a camp would be assigned. Meanwhile the Colonel caused guards to be thrown out around the regiment, lest some depredations might be committed in the town for which he would be censured and held responsible.

In the morning General Hurlbut visited the regiment, and jokingly inquired of the Colonel what regiment of prisoners he was guarding? At an early hour the regiment moved into the camp designated, near the city, and thereafter reported to Colonel M. K. Lawler, then commanding the Post of Jackson. The time at this station was spent by the regiment in drilling, performing post and picket duty and learning certain things concerning military life not inculcated in the schooling at Camp Fuller. Severe orders were received here from superior head-quarters, prohibiting soldiers from committing depredations of any kind, entering the yards and premises of citizens, and being absent from the encampment without proper authority. One day a member of the Ninety-fifth, unmindful of the strict regulations in force, happened to wander some distance from camp, for the purpose of procuring certain articles of nourishment not usually issued by the army commissaries — articles which did not really belong to him, but which he thought might be collected without injury to any loyal individual, and with gratification to his own appetite and that of his companions in camp. While out on this expedition he suddenly found himself surprised by an individual claiming to be one of "Jackson's Confederate cavalry," and who at once demanded the immediate and unconditional surrender of the astonished Union soldier. Seeing himself overpowered he complyingly delivered himself up. The captor, however, informed the prisoner that if he would reveal his name, company and regiment, and give information as to the number and disposition of the Federal forces then encamped at Jackson, also the name of the commanding general, he could be released and allowed to return to camp. Little suspecting the real military character of the captor, and not having enlisted in the service for the purpose of conveying important intelligence or rendering aid and comfort to the enemy, the steadfast devotee of Uncle Samuel gave a most cunning and glowing account of the number and disposition of the Union army at Jackson, which information was characterized more for intended exaggeration than entire truthfulness. It turned out that the supposed Confederate cavalryman was none other than a disguised Federal, whom the commanding general had sent out for the purpose of looking after stragglers, and soon afterward an order was received at regimental head-quarters from Major General Hurlbut, directing that "the soldier of the Ninety-fifth who strayed away from camp on Sunday, and met, as he says, one of Jackson's Confederate cavalry, be kept on bread and water three (3) days, and perform three (3) days hard labor, for the offense of leaving camp lines without proper permission or orders:" which punishment the commanding officer of the regiment caused to be carried into effect.

The command was to remain in camp at Jackson only a few days, when it would be hurried forward to the front, where preparations were already going on in the army under General Grant for an active campaign in the field. The regiment had as yet experienced little of the fatigues and onerous duties incident to war; had made no marches of any length loaded down with knapsacks, blankets, haversacks, guns and accoutrements, and as it was soon to be called upon to perform such tasks, the commanding officer thought best to practice in that kind of drill preparatory to leaving Jackson. Accordingly, one day the regiment was ordered out for a march, fully armed and accoutred, which, in the army, is well understood to include all the military appendages and implements carried by a soldier. The direction taken was on one of the main roads leading from the city, and the day chosen was of the sultriest kind, though in the month of November. The men, with their well-filled, heavy knapsacks strapped upon their backs, moved along the route for a short distance with ease and without a murmur, but as the advance continued, the burdens upon their persons grew weightier and weightier, and they now began to fully realize the irksomeness produced by being obliged to carry knapsacks several hours and miles in succession. The commanding officer continued the march a few miles into the country, and having proceeded a distance sufficiently satisfactory to all concerned, countermarched to camp, the regiment being greatly fatigued, and the men not being very favorably disposed to a repetition of "Colonel Tom's knapsack drill."

On the twenty-first day of November, 1862, the regiment proceeded by railroad to Grand Junction, Tennessee, in accordance with orders from General Hurlbut, with instructions to report to Brigadier General Hamilton, then commanding the left wing 13th Army Corps, Army and Department of the Tennessee. On arriving there, it was immediately assigned to Brigadier General John McArthur's Division of this corps, and was conducted into camp by one of his staff officers, who met the regiment at the dêpot for that purpose. The Ninety-fifth was the first new regiment under the President's last call for troops to enter this division of the old army, and was now called upon to associate, drill, march, fight and compete with those veteran regiments, which, entering the service at the beginning of the war, had fought nobly and won laurels in the hotly contested battles of Belmont, Wilson's Creek, Fort Donelson, Shiloh, Corinth, Iuka and Hatchie. The division of General McArthur at this time was composed of some of the oldest and best troops sent to the field from the States of Illinois, Wisconsin, Iowa, and Kansas. The Eleventh, Twelfth and Seventeenth Illinois, the Fourteenth, Sixteenth and Seventeenth Wisconsin, the Eleventh, Thirteenth, Fifteenth and Sixteenth Iowa, and the First Kansas regiments belonged to it, and had already made their mark in the war against secession and rebellion. Their ranks had been thinned by the casualties of battle and the service, and their regimental organizations had thereby become reduced far below the minimum standard.

The advent of a new, full regiment among them was therefore a matter of curiosity with these battle-scarred and war-experienced veterans. They were anxious to see how the raw recruits, just down from the North, would conduct themselves in camp life; anxious to scrutinize their movements on dress-parade and drill, supposing the regiment had as yet obtained little knowledge of such matters. On the evening of Nov. 21st, as the Ninety-fifth passed from the cars at Grand Junction, and wended their way through the various encampments to its own, the old soldiers gathered along its route to witness the big regiment. So long had it been since they had seen a full one, that many of them wanted to know what brigade was passing? Late in the evening the regiment reached its camping-grounds, and was welcomed by the excellent brass band of Colonel Deitzler's Brigade, who cheered up the boys with patriotic music. On the following day, the regiment was assigned to the 1st Brigade of General McArthur's Division, commanded by Colonel George W. Deitzler of the 1st Kansas Infantry — afterward Brigadier General of Volunteers. Thus was completed its incorporation into the grand Army of the Tennessee, then preparing for a general forward movement, under the direction of Major General Grant, against the enemy in Northern Mississippi.

Attached now to one of the best fighting divisions in the army, the task before it was to establish and build up a good military character, of which the division might be proud, and which would make the organization an ornament and honor to the service and country. Soon after getting settled in this camp, the regiment resumed its dress-parades, and the appearance of the new command in such an act attracted a crowd of military observers and critics, who were curious to know how these inexperienced troops would perform. The general commanding the division was also present, and desired to learn of what material the regiment consisted. He and all others in attendance were highly satisfied and astonished to see with what precision and uniformity the new levies executed the different movements. A few days afterward the whole division was ordered out on drill, where a dozen regiments, several batteries of artillery and a battalion of cavalry were to maneuvre together at the commands of the general. On this occasion the Ninety-fifth, for the first time in its military existence, took part in an exercise of this character, and acquitted itself with credit, obtaining particular praise from the general commanding. During this same drill, the regiments were all sweeping up over the wide field and passing the general in line of battle. As the Ninety-fifth approached with steady step and unbroken line, he glanced along the well-guided ranks with admiration; and remarked that the Ninety-fifth need n't be called a *new* regiment any longer, it was *old enough* for the service. Thus at the outset the regiment won golden opinions from old officers and soldiers. The drilling and constant preparation for such scenes while in camp at Rockford and Jackson, now produced the good results of such training, and the organization, in its efficient and well-disciplined condition, was considered a valuable acquisition to the brigade and division.

The regiment, at the time of leaving the State, was unprovided with tents of any kind, and after arriving at Jackson was unable to procure any except the small shelter, or as the soldiers were wont to call them, "*dog* or *pup* tents." These were deemed a great nuisance, as they had to be pitched close upon the ground, and none but the very shortest men could sleep beneath them unexposed to the weather. On reaching Grand Junction it was observed that other regiments were well supplied, and made comfortable with the large wall-tents, and Colonel Humphrey, always solicitous for the welfare of his men, determined that this matter should be remedied in his own command, if possible. He accordingly invited General McArthur to visit his camp one day, for the purpose of witnessing the practical workings of the shelter-tent. Preparatory to the general's inspection, the colonel, employing a little strategy, caused one of the tents to be pitched in front of his head-quarters, and arranged with a man over six feet high, the tallest soldier in the regiment, that he should be lying in it, stretched to his fullest length, at the general's approach. It was utterly impossible for a man of such proportions as the soldier selected, to occupy the tent without constantly having the head and feet exposed. The general, on witnessing this ludicrous scene, expressed his displeasure at such contracted provision for the men of his command, and assured the colonel that larger accommodations should be at once provided. Soon afterward, the condemned shelter-tents were all turned over, and the regiment supplied with the same kind as the other troops.

The stay at Camp No. Three, Grand Junction, was short, and soon General Grant ordered forward the whole Army of the Tennessee, then collected at this point, at LaGrange, and near Memphis, against the enemy, reported to be in force near the Tallahatchie river, in the State of Mississippi. It was expected the rebels would offer battle, and contest the passage at that point.

CHAPTER III.

The Movement from Grand Junction — A tedious Day's March — Fatigue of the Men — Iron Accessions to Knapsacks — Crossing the Tallahatchie — Halt at Abbeville — Advance to Yockena — News of Van Dorn's Raid into Holly Springs — Return of the Army — Expedition to Salem, Miss. — Anecdote of a Jug — March of the Regiment to Memphis.

AT an early hour on the morning of November 26th, 1862, the camps were aroused at Grand Junction by the familiar reveille, tents struck, knapsacks packed, coffee and hard-cracker partaken of, and everything made ready for a seasonable departure. Following the practice instituted at Camp Fuller, the Ninety-fifth made bonfires of boxes, barrels, mess tables and other camp furniture for which there was no transportation, and which were of no further military importance. There were no barracks at this point for the troops, and no occasion was, therefore, offered for the happening of mischievousness similar to that which has already been related in connection with the return of the regiment to camp from the dêpot at Rockford, Illinois. The custom of disposing by fire of all articles and rubbish of old camps prevails universally in the army, and whatever the soldier has used in camp for his own comfort, if it cannot be transported at the time of moving, must suffer unceremonious consignment to the devouring flames, or be otherwise destroyed. In other words, nothing useful to a human being in rebeldom must at such times be left behind to fall into the enemy's hands for his aid and comfort. The route taken by this portion of General Grant's army was through the northern part of the State of Mississippi, moving on the road leading to Holly Springs, Abbeville and Oxford. After the decisive battles of Shiloh and the seige of Corinth, the Confederates had retreated to their new line of operations and thrown up strong fortifications on the south side of the Tallahatchie river, a short distance north of Abbeville. The main traveled road and the Mississippi Central Railroad crossed the river at this point, and here General Pemberton was stationed in force, to resist the passage of the large Federal army which was now sweeping forward, with the rebel stronghold on the Tallahatchie as the objective point.

The first day's march out from Grand Junction was long and tedious, continuing far into the night before bivouacking. The distance traveled must have been full twenty-five miles. Some of the men, overcome with fatigue and troubled with sore feet, were obliged to fall out of the ranks and come up afterward as best they could. This was the first real march the regiment had ever undertaken, and it was not expected that they would perform it with the same endurance as those who were enured to such duty by long service in the field. Yet a small number only was found absent from roll-call after arriving in camp that night, though all were tired, sorefooted and hungry, and well prepared for relishing the contents of their haversacks and for the enjoyment of sleep.

The men, before starting from camp that morning, had filled their knapsacks to their fullest capacity, putting in articles and material more weighty than old soldiers would have deemed advisable under the circumstances. For a few miles these burdens seemed light, the march progressed lively, and the boys were cheerful and talkative, even to witticism. Now and then along the road horse-shoes were discovered which had been relieved from further duty on the hoof, and a few of the men, disliking to pass by and abandon such articles, undertook to transport a number of them, thinking they would be productive of good luck, and be useful, perhaps, to some one in the future. The knapsacks, increased in weight by such metallic accessions, grew heavier and more irksome, until finally the horse-shoes were willingly cast away, and the question began to be seriously agitated whether the regulation bulk of the knapsack itself should not be overhauled, lightened and materially decreased, retaining little else therein except what was actually needful on the march.

On the following day the march was resumed, and the column moved on through Holly Springs and seven miles beyond, to near Lumpkin's Mills, where the whole army halted for the night. There were now indications that we were nearing the enemy, as there had been lively skirmishing by our cavalry in front, and the occasional booming of artillery suggested that active work might be at hand. We were only a few miles from the Tallahatchie, where the main force of the enemy was supposed to be, and the Federal column rested in camp, November 28th, with orders to regimental commanders to keep their men well in hand, while the First Kansas and the Eleventh Illinois, of Colonel Deitzler's brigade, made a reconnoisance in the direction of the crossing at the river, felt of the enemy and ascertained his position, preparatory to a general engagement. On the 29th, information was received that the enemy was evacuating his fortifications at the Tallahatchie, and General Grant ordered his army forward immediately. General McArthur's was the advance division, and Colonel Deitzler's the advance brigade. The column moved in the afternoon of that day, and the advance arrived at the recently evacuated fort on the north side of the river after dark, the Ninety-fifth being the second regiment of infantry to occupy it. The bridge at this point had been burned by the retreating rebels, and only the Eleventh Illinois Infantry, and companies "A" and "F," of the Ninety-fifth, succeeded in crossing on the remaining stringers. The cavalry had already forded the stream and passed on in pursuit of the enemy. The bridge had to be repaired before the artillery and army wagons could pass over, and the army was delayed here for that purpose until the following day. That night, therefore, the Ninety-fifth bivouacked around the fort, on the north side of the river, except the two companies mentioned, which crossed the river and occupied the works there. Officers and men lay down to sleep behind the large trees which had been felled by the Confederates to give their artillery range, and during the night heavy details from the regiment were busy at work on the bridge. The work was continued all night long, and early on the following day (30th,) it was in readiness for the army to cross.

It was here ascertained from deserters and prisoners that Pemberton had evacuated only a few hours previous to the arrival of the Federal advance, taking with him a force of twenty or twenty-five thousand men. The smoking cinders of the bridge and the appearance of the fortifications indicated that he had not been long absent.

The rebel position here was well selected and strongly fortified naturally and artificially. Had the enemy accepted an engagement there, the slaughter of an attacking column must necessarily have been terrible, as its course would have been through swamps to an opening near the river bank, upon which the enemy could have concentrated a most deadly fire.

But there were other important movements progressing at the same time on the enemy's left flank, under direction of the quick-moving Sherman, which undoubtedly decided the evacuation by the rebels of their defenses on the Tallahatchie. This flank movement was being executed by General Sherman simultaneously with the arrival of General McArthur's division at the bridge. He threw his command across the river at a fordable point some miles below the fort, and was in condition to move around and attack the enemy's position from the rear. Pemberton discovered the trap being set to "gobble" his entire force, and before the strategical movement could be consummated, withdrew his army and retreated hastily in the direction of and beyond Grenada.

On the 30th of November, the Federal forces, delayed by the repairing of the bridge over the Tallahatchie, moved forward, the Ninety-fifth being in advance of all the infantry. The regiment arrived at Abbeville, four miles distant, at noon, drenched in a terrible rain storm. Here most of the command took shelter in the deserted houses and sheds which that secession village afforded. The rebel army having retreated precipitately beyond Grenada, and in the direction of Jackson, Miss., pursued closely by our cavalry, gave no further signs of standing and offering battle to the advancing Union columns. The chase on the part of our infantry was, therefore, slackened at Abbeville, and the Ninety-fifth went into camp two miles south-east of the town. The regiment here furnished large details of men to repair the Mississippi Central Railroad bridge over the Tallahatchie, which was partially destroyed by the rebels in their hasty evacuation and flight. In a few days the new work was completed, and trains came through regularly from Holly Springs. The regiment remained in camp at Abbeville until the 18th day of December, 1862, performing various kinds of post duty.

The men had now seen something of active service in the field, and learned from experience some of the ways and customs of the army. At the time of starting out from Grand Junction, they were looked upon by older soldiers as raw, inexperienced recruits, though it was confessed they had exhibited on drill and parade a good degree of military discipline and knowledge. In camp they had shown themselves superb soldiers, as universally admitted, and it remained to see how the new organization would conduct itself, and hold out in the trying time of a long and rapid march. The regiment had therefore entered upon the present campaign, with the idea prominent among some of the old troops that *they* only were completely adequate for the lengthy march before them, and the regiment, on the other hand, entertained the belief that it could march as fast and as far in a day as any other regiment, old or new. The veteran soldiers, during this campaign, took occasion to confer upon the new levies the appellation of "forty-dollar men," suggestive of the forty-dollar bounty which each recruit had received from his county, in consideration of his enlistment. But after a few days' marching, in which it was noticed that the Ninety-fifth always kept well closed up in the column, and came into camp at night with but few stragglers behind, the men of the old regiments were compelled to alter their opinions materially, and the clamor about "forty-dollar men" finally subsided.

After remaining at Abbeville a number of days, the army moved on through Oxford, and the Ninety-fifth arrived at Yockena Station on the 18th of December, 1862. Here news came that the rebel General Van Dorn had made a dash with his cavalry into Holly Springs, surprised and mostly captured the Federal garrison, and destroyed large quantities of quartermaster and commissary stores belonging to the Federal Government. Holly Springs was then a dêpot of supplies for General Grant's army, and was therefore an important point in his line of communication. This bold and unexpected dash of Van Dorn had much to do with changing the character and destination of the campaign. It may be inferred that the sudden appearance of Van Dorn was unexpected. General Grant, however, was fully advised of that rebel leader's whereabouts,—knew that he was hovering around Holly Springs, awaiting a favorable opportunity to attack the place, and, to prevent the occurrence of this threatening disaster, in due time telegraphed this information to the commandant of that Post, warning him to be on his guard, and keep sharp lookout for Van Dorn. The Post commander failed to provide for the emergency, and one morning at an early hour found himself and the most of his garrison in the hands of the cunning Confederate Chief. As soon as this intelligence reached the main Federal army, near Yockena, it was immediately ordered to return to Holly Springs. The countermarch from Yockena commenced December 19th, and the same day the Ninety-fifth marched back to its former camp, near Abbeville. On the 20th the march was resumed at an early hour, and the regiment arrived in Holly Springs at ten o'clock, P. M., of that day, having made one of the longest and most tedious forced marches which it ever experienced in the service.

The army halted at this place for several days, and on the day following our arrival, Colonel Deitzler's Brigade, composed of the First Kansas, Sixteenth Wisconsin, and Ninety-fifth Illinois Infantry, and a battery, was ordered on an expedition to Salem, Miss., fifteen miles east of Holly Springs, for the purpose of intercepting Van Dorn, who was still reported in that vicinity. The regiments took three days' rations, started early and arrived at Salem in the afternoon of the same day. The command halted here one day, awaiting the approach of the enemy, and Colonel Deitzler, after advancing a few miles beyond Salem, learning that Van Dorn had passed south a short time previous to our coming, and was now well out of reach, and pursuit of cavalry by infantry being useless, moved his brigade back to Salem, and returned with it to Holly Springs on the 23rd of December. There were very severe orders on this short expedition in reference to the soldiers entering dwelling-houses and yards by the roadside, forbidding the taking of chickens and vegetables, and against jay-hawking generally. Nevertheless, the boys could not see the propriety of passing through an enemy's country without, in a measure, collecting supplies, and as they had been provided with short rations for the trip, the orders were somewhat evaded, and many a soldier marched into Salem with a fowl of some description slung over his shoulder.

The First Kansas Infantry was one of the best fighting regiments in the service, and had acquired something of a reputation also for appropriating things to their own use, in which, really, they could not be said to have had a clear and unencumbered ownership. It may be asserted with safety that when there was anything good to eat which could be seized near the route of march, the First Kansas was in no fear of starvation. On this expedition, as usual, it did not suffer for want of fowl and other meat, and the Ninety-fifth, though not so bold because not so experienced in this peculiar branch of the service as their compeers of the First Kansas, yet were making rapid progress in learning the skillful *modus operandi* of bringing eatables into camp, and were well provided with the various luxuries afforded by the country. At Salem, cornmeal, sugar and syrup were found in considerable abundance, and, notwithstanding the prohibitory orders on the subject, those soldiers of jay-hawking propensities (of which there are some in every regiment,) laid in a good store of these necessities.

One day two men belonging to the Ninety-fifth, were noticed by the brigade commander to be approaching camp, conveying a large jug suspended on a pole, which gave rise to the suspicion that the contents thereof was contraband—such as milk, honey, or syrup, and had been surreptitiously obtained, against the orders in such case provided. The suspicious parties were therefore at once arrested and brought under guard to Colonel Deitzler's head-quarters for examination and punishment. On arriving there the colonel ascertained with surprise, but to the great merriment of the parties implicated, and other soldiers who stood around, that the earthen vessel in question contained nothing but pure, unadulterated water, which the soldiers had obtained at a neighboring spring. The colonel acknowledged himself sold, and the boys proceeded on their way to camp, rejoicing.

A few days after the return of this expedition to Holly Springs, General Grant's army took up its line of march for Memphis, starting soon after Christmas, 1862. The Ninety-fifth arrived at Moscow, Tenn.,—a small town between LaGrange and Memphis,—December 30th, and on the following day mustered for pay at that place. On the first day of January, 1863, it resumed the march, and on the 2nd, arrived at Collierville. Colonel Deitzler's brigade was ordered to halt here a few days prior to advancing to Memphis, during which time the regiments were mainly occupied in repairing and guarding the railroad, doing picket and other duties. While remaining at this place, the regiments were required to be up and in line of battle at three o'clock, A. M., for several mornings in succession, watching for the enemy until daylight. This precaution was taken to prevent surprise by the enemy, who was known to be hovering on the rear and flanks of the withdrawing Union army. The disaster which had occurred at Holly Springs made all commanders more watchful thereafter, and the troops were kept on the alert, and well in hand, day and night, for any emergency. On the 13th of January the brigade moved forward toward Memphis, arrived there in the afternoon, and went into camp three miles out from the city.

The campaign thus closed in Northern Mississippi, though successful in driving the enemy from his base on the Tallahatchie river, yet had not effected all the objects originally planned. Pemberton with his army had been compelled to evacuate his strong position, and beat a hasty retreat far into the interior, but he was still unconquered. Whether the grand march from Grand Junction and LaGrange, southward, was instituted with a view of eventually attacking and taking Vicksburg from the rear, *via* Grenada and Jackson, Mississippi, and was discontinued on account of impracticability, or for other reasons, was best understood by the great military man who then stood at the head of the Western Army, planned its campaigns, and altered at discretion its sweeping course of march. It was soon evident, however, that there was a grand expedition on foot for the Army of the Tennessee, that the campaign was to be continued, and that it would be prosecuted with renewed vigor down the Mississippi Valley, against Vicksburg, though in midwinter.

CHAPTER IV.

Expedition from Memphis down the River against Vicksburg — Arrival at Milliken's Bend — The Canal near Young's Point — Colonel Deitzler's Brigade ordered to Lake Providence — Important order affecting the Ninety-fifth — The Canal at Lake Providence — Sickness and Death in the Regiment — Raising of Colored Regiments — Policy of the Government concerning Slavery during the Rebellion, reviewed — Resignation of Colonel Church — March of the Army from Milliken's Bend to "Hard Times" Landing — Ninety-fifth transferred to General Ransom's Brigade — Crossing to Grand Gulf — March to rear of Vicksburg — Charges of 19th and 22nd of May — The Siege — Surrender of the City — General Ransom's Brigade sent to Natchez — Its operations while there — Its return to Vicksburg.

SIMULTANEOUSLY with the presence of General Grant's army at Memphis, a large fleet of transports was also collecting at that point for the purpose of conveying the troops down the river to operate against Vicksburg. These were ready by the 19th of January for the reception of General McArthur's division, which was now designated as the 6th Division of the 17th Army Corps, commanded by Major General James B. McPherson, changes in corps organizations having occurred at Memphis. On that day the Ninety-fifth embarked upon the steamer "Maria Denning," a very capacious but aged craft, which had grown old in a long service on the Mississippi waters.

The Eleventh Regiment Iowa Infantry, Eighteenth Wisconsin, and a company of the Second Illinois Artillery also embarked on this boat at the same time, and every nook and corner of the yet staunch old *tub* was filled above with soldiers, and crammed full below decks with horses, mules, army wagons and artillery. All who have soldiered it are well acquainted with the delay and tediousness attendant upon the embarkation of an army upon steamboats, and all members of the Ninety-fifth well remember. that this at Memphis was one of that nature, the regiment having remained at the levee, standing in the mud from morning until afternoon before getting aboard. No one complained, however, every inconvenience being considered a military necessity. Finally the troops were loaded, one long whistle sounded from General McArthur's flag-boat, "Platte Valley," as signal for starting, the splendid fleet of fifteen steamers swung out into the stream, and were soon steaming down the river, and wending their course toward the subsequent scene of busy military operations around the "Hill City" of the South. The fleet landed each day before dark, lying by nights, and arrived at Milliken's Bend, fifteen miles above Vicksburg, on the 26th of January. The troops disembarked on the following day, going into camp near the levee. It was a few miles below this encampment where the celebrated canal was being dug, which was intended to turn the channel of the Mississippi sufficiently to admit transports and gunboats, and thus gain river communication below the city of Vicksburg.

Major General Sherman, a few weeks previous, had ascended the Yazoo river with a large force, effected a landing near Chickasaw Bluffs, and stormed the strong line of the enemy's works at that point, with the object of gaining a base near the river communication on the north side of Vicksburg. This expedition failed in accomplishing its purpose, though not without great gallantry displayed on the part of the attacking Union columns. The canal at Young's Point was next resorted to as a practicable means of flanking Vicksburg, and the numerous batteries lining its bluffs, and of obtaining a base of operations at some point on the river below that stronghold. The river makes a short bend near Young's Point, and just below, on the east side, sat the haughty city of Vicksburg, bidding defiance from her bluffy heights to the near approach and passage of Federal transports and gunboats. The Ninety-fifth, soon after arriving near Young's Point, aided in the construction of the canal, furnishing details of men day and night for that purpose. Colonel Deitzler's brigade, however, remained here but a short time, and was soon ordered up the river to initiate the digging of another canal at Lake Providence. Before starting on this trip, an important order, affecting the standing of the Ninety-fifth, was issued by the brigade commander, and I take the liberty of introducing the same here, deeming it will be read with interest by all surviving members of the organization. It is as follows, and explains itself:

HEAD-QUARTERS 1ST BRIG., 6TH DIV., 17TH ARMY CORPS,
Camp near Young's Point, La., *Jan.* 30*th*, 1863.

SPECIAL ORDERS, NO. 6.

Paragraph IV, Special Orders Number Five, from these Headquarters, imposing a fine of ten dollars each on certain men of the Ninety-fifth Illinois Infantry, having accomplished the end for which it was issued, is hereby revoked.

The colonel commanding takes this occasion to compliment the officers and men of the Ninety-fifth regiment for their excellent discipline. The soldierly bearing and conduct of a very large majority of the men of said regiment, have always been above reproach, but it must be confessed that there were a few reckless and refractory spirits, whose unmilitary and ungentlemanly practices, in defiance of regulations and orders, had a very demoralizing tendency, and would, if not checked, result in giving to the whole regiment an unenviable reputation. The stringent orders issued and enforced to remedy such irregularities, have had their desired effect; the Ninety-fifth stands at the head of the list in the brigade, if not in the division, in point of good order and discipline, and "a patient continuance in well-doing," which is certain to bring its reward in any position of life, will ensure the regiment a bright record, to which they can point with pride.

By order of
GEORGE W. DEITZLER,
S. T. SMITH, *Col. Com'ng 1st Brigade.*
Capt. and A. A. A. Gen'l.

The regiment came up the river, and landed at Lake Providence, La., on the second day of February, 1863. Colonel Deitzler's brigade went into camp there, being the first troops, and for some days the only ones, sent to that place. The work to be performed here was the cutting of a canal from the Mississippi river to the small and beautiful lake, a half mile distant, whose level was much below that of the river at a high stage of water. At this season of the year the banks of the Mississippi were full. The lake was made by waters from the great stream which swept so near to it, and had certain outlets or bayous running in the direction of, and almost connecting with the Washita river, which empties into the Red river some miles above the mouth of the latter. It was supposed that on letting the waters of the Mississippi into Lake Providence by a canal, the principal of these bayous receiving the flood would be widened and deepened to such an extent as to allow gunboats and river transports to pass through, and convey the army under General Grant to some available point on the Mississippi, below the city of Vicksburg. The great question of the campaign seemed to be, how was the defiant fortress of the rebellion in the Southwest to be got at or around, since it could not be attacked and carried from the river front without immense loss of life. The question was solved only by the persevering genius and moving spirit of the campaign, in those attempts and experiments which were carried on under his direct supervision, and which finally resulted in such glorious success to the national arms.

On the day after the arrival of the Ninety-fifth at Lake Providence, the work on the canal was commenced, and large details were made daily on the regiment for that duty. Most of the labor performed on this work was done by Colonel Deitzler's brigade, though the whole of the Seventeenth Army Corps subsequently came up from Young's Point, and camped at and near the lake.

About the middle of the month of February the canal was completed and ready for conducting a large volume of the Mississippi, then in a high stage, into the calm and beautiful lake near by. Nothing remained but to cut the levee, and then the irresistible waters rushed through, deepening and widening the channel as they foamed onward, seeking their level in the sleeping lake, in the bayous beyond, and in the low lands for miles around. In a few days the high banks of the lake were filled to overflowing, numerous plantations were flooded, the village of Lake Providence itself was submerged, and the different encampments of troops endangered by the rising waters. The father of waters, loosened from its barriers, was on a rampage through Lake Providence. The experiment was now tried of entering steamboats into the lake through the canal. None, however, attempted the feat except a small screw-steamer of light draught, by the name of "Rawlins," and the channel never became of sufficient depth to admit the larger transports. The "Rawlins," therefore, had a fine time of it, scudding from point to point in the lake, and doing business between the camps which dotted either shore. The bayou through which communication was intended from the lake did not widen and deepen sufficiently for the reception of large-sized steamboats, though the different pioneer corps of the army had been busily employed clearing it of old logs and rubbish prior to the introduction of the waters. This attempt, therefore, to open a new communication to the Mississippi below Vicksburg was abandoned as impracticable, though it was not without its good effects in hurting the rebellion and advancing the cause of the Union in the campaign then progressing. The whole country back from Lake Providence for hundreds of miles into the interior of Louisiana — a section prolific of rebels and abounding in all the various supplies which that genial clime and fertile soil produced — had been overflown and desolated by the flood which the canal had brought in from the Mississippi river. It was a portion of country whence the Confederacy east of the Mississippi obtained large quantities of subsistence for its army, and if the canal turned out to be of no other importance, it at least struck a heavy blow at the rebellion by drowning out and despoiling many of these means of supply. Meanwhile the canal at Young's Point met with similar ill success; both were abandoned, and immediately other plans were projected to accomplish the object they had failed to effect.

The encampment of the Ninety-fifth, while at Lake Providence, was located upon low grounds near the levee and the canal. It occupied the same camp from the time of landing there, on the 2nd of February, 1863, until the commencement of the grand movement of General Grant's army from Milliken's Bend,

La., in the latter part of the following April. During this period much sickness prevailed in the regiment, and its hospital building in the village was crowded with the sick soldiers, who, worn down by the fatigues of the active duties performed since entering the service, were passing through acclimation, and were now overtaken by the afflictive hand of prostrating disease. The cases of sickness increased for a time with frightful rapidity, though every precaution was taken, and means employed to prevent its alarming prevalence. Deaths became of frequent occurrence; the muffled drum, with its mournful roll, beating time to the familiar dead-march, gave notice almost daily that the corpse of some Union soldier was being consigned to the burial ground near by — to an early grave in the low, wet soil at Lake Providence. Yet disease, sickness and death were not confined to the Ninety-fifth alone. Other troops who entered the service at about the same time, experienced their full share of these inconveniences, while the old soldiers, having become fully acclimated to the Southern climate, fared much better. All regiments, at a certain period after entering the service, are required to pass through such an ordeal of sickness. There are certain diseases which the majority of a regiment are bound to experience. Some are carried away by them, or rendered unfit for further duty in the army, while many, possessing those strong constitutions bestowed by nature, adapted for encountering the rough trials of military life, come forth with renewed and rugged health, and seem better prepared than ever to execute the tasks set before them.

While the Seventeenth Army Corps was encamped at Providence, the new policy of the Government in organizing and arming negroes for military duty was carried into effect. Soon after the arrival of Colonel Deitzler's brigade at this place, large numbers of colored people flocked in from the surrounding country responsive to President Lincoln's Proclamation, issued on the 22nd day of September, 1862, which, on the failure of the States in rebellion to comply with its conditions, namely, to lay down their arms and return to their allegiance, was to be carried into effect on and after January 1st, 1863. As is well known, the proclamation was not accepted or complied with on the part of the rebels except in few localities in the Confederacy, and accordingly the population of African descent embraced the opportunity whenever it was possible, of fleeing from their old masters and swarming into the Union lines for protection. It was claimed by some people, and there are probably those who still adhere to the opinion, that the war against secession was carried on by the Government from the beginning with the prominent idea on the part of the Administration of abolishing slavery in the States where it existed, and that the incipient plan of emancipating the slaves was fully illustrated and carried into practice by the Proclamation of President Lincoln which freed and authorized the arming of the negroes. To show the fallacy of this misconceived notion, the military action and policy of the Government relative to the subject of slavery, as announced in the acts of Congress, in different orders from the War Department, and from various commanding generals in the field, may be referred to as a recorded and complete refutation of the accusation, and an unanswerable argument that the final edict of emancipation was issued only after a series of attempts on the part of the Federal Government to avoid it by constant appeals to rebels in arms to return to their allegiance, and was proclaimed only as a *war measure* to hurt traitors and kill rebellion.

When General Fremont, in the very beginning of the war, assumed to receive negro fugitives fleeing to his army from the plantations of Missouri, and decreed their freedom, an order from Washington immediately informed him that his action was disapproved, and that all such fugitives coming into the Union lines should be returned to their owners, or at least be prohibited from seeking refuge and remaining within the Federal encampments. The same line of policy was marked out plainly for commanding officers to pursue in dealing with slavery in other portions of the United States, showing conclusively that it was not the desire or intention of the Government to molest or interfere with the domestic institutions of any State. The States in rebellion did not appreciate or profit by this forbearing, lenient and *coaxing* treatment of the General Government, and long afterward, in 1862, the policy of the Federal Administration was necessarily changed to more vigorous measures against the rebellion and its handmaid, slavery, as demanded by the stern necessities of the times. The following extracts from an order issued by General Grant, while at Corinth, Miss., in August, 1862, show plainly that even at that stage of the contest the object of the war was not the general emancipation of negroes in the South, nor to meddle with the peculiar institution, except to receive and employ those fugitives who came into the camps as laborers, in the capacity of teamsters, cooks and servants. It was as follows:

HEAD-QUARTERS DISTRICT OF WEST TENNESSEE, }
Corinth, Miss., August 11th, 1862. }

GENERAL ORDERS, No. 72.

Recent acts of Congress prohibit the army from returning fugitives from labor to their claimants, and authorize the employment of such persons in the service of the Government. The following orders are, therefore, published for the guidance of the army in the military district in this matter:

I. All fugitives thus employed must be registered, the names of the fugitives and claimants given, and must be borne upon the morning reports of the command in which they are kept, showing how they are employed.

II. Fugitive slaves may be employed as laborers in the Quartermaster's, Subsistence or Engineer departments, and whenever by such employment a soldier may be saved to the ranks. They may be employed as teamsters, as company cooks — not exceeding four to a company — or as hospital attendants and nurses. Officers may employ them as private servants, in which latter case the fugitives will not be paid or rationed by the Government. Negroes not thus employed will be deemed unauthorized persons, and must be excluded from camp.

III. Officers and soldiers are positively prohibited from enticing slaves to leave their masters. When it becomes necessary to employ this kind of labor, commanding officers of posts or troops must send details — always under the charge of a suitable commissioned officer — to press into the service the slaves of disloyal persons, to the number required.

* * * * * * * * *

By command of
MAJOR GENERAL U. S. GRANT.

JOHN A. RAWLINS,
Assistant Adjutant General.

This rule of military action in reference to slavery was rigidly adhered to and carried out in General Grant's campaign through Northern Mississippi, in December, 1862, and up to February of the following year, the time when his troops were encamped at Lake Providence. President Lincoln's proclamation of September, 1862, stated:

"That hereafter, as heretofore, the war will be prosecuted for the object of practically restoring the constitutional relation between the United States and each of the States and the people thereof, in which States that relation is or may be suspended or disturbed. That it was his purpose, upon the next meeting of Congress, to again recommend the adoption of a practical measure tendering pecuniary aid to the free acceptance or rejection of all slave States so called, the people whereof may not then be in rebellion against the United States, and which States may then have voluntarily adopted, or thereafter may voluntarily adopt immediate or gradual abolishment of slavery within their respective limits; and that the effort to colonize persons of African descent, with their consent, upon this continent, or elsewhere, with the previously obtained consent of the government existing there, will be continued. That on the 1st day of January, in the year of our Lord one thousand eight hundred and sixty-three, all persons held as slaves within any State or designated part of a State, the people whereof shall then be in rebellion against the United States, shall be thenceforward and forever free; and the executive government of the United States, including the military and naval authority thereof, will recognize and maintain the freedom of such persons, and will do no act to repress such persons, or any of them, in any effort they may make for their actual freedom. That the Executive will, on the first day of January, aforesaid, by proclamation, designate the States and parts of States, if any, in which the people thereof respectively shall then be in rebellion against the United States; and the fact that any State, or the people thereof, shall on that day be in good faith represented in the Congress of the United States, by members chosen thereto at elections wherein a majority of the qualified voters of such State shall have participated, shall, in the absence of strong countervailing testimony be deemed conclusive evidence that such State and the people thereof are not then in rebellion against the United States."

Meanwhile the seceded States spurned this offer of remuneration and guaranty of property in case of their return to loyalty, and up to the first day of January, 1863, no proposition was ever heard of from any of them, no action was ever taken on their part indicating a desire to resume their relations to the Union, upon the liberal terms proposed. The rebellion continued. The war was prosecuted in all its rigor, and on the first day of January, 1863, the chief executive of the nation, in fulfillment of what he had previously declared, and from which the South had had long opportunity to escape, sent forth the celebrated fiat of emancipation, carrying freedom to millions of human beings theretofore employed in the interests of the Confederacy, and striking a death-blow at the head and front of the rebellion itself. After reciting the substance of his September proclamation, he declared as follows:

"Now, therefore, I, Abraham Lincoln, President of the United States, by virtue of the power in me vested as commander-in-chief of the army and navy of the United States, and as a fit and necessary war measure for suppressing said rebellion, do, on this first day of January, in the year of our Lord one thousand eight hundred and sixty-three, and in accordance with my purpose so to do publicly proclaimed for the full period of one hundred days from the day first above mentioned, order and designate as the States and parts of States wherein the people thereof respectively are this day in rebellion against the United States, the following, to wit: *   *   *   *   *   And by virtue of the power and for the purpose aforesaid, I do order and declare that all persons held as slaves within said designated States and parts of States, are and henceforward shall be free; and that the Executive Government of the United States, including the military and naval authorities thereof, will recognize and maintain the freedom of said persons. And I further declare and make known, that such persons, of suitable condition, will be received into the armed service of the United States, to garrison forts, positions, stations and other places, and to man vessels of all sorts in said service. And upon this act, sincerely believed to be an act of justice, warranted by the Constitution upon military necessity, I invoke the considerate judgment of mankind and the gracious favor of Almighty God."

In the early part of the year 1863, the third year of the rebellion, the organization of negro troops began at Lake Providence, in accordance with the policy of the Government thus declared. Adjutant General Thomas came on a mission from Washington to inaugurate the new movement, and arrived at Lake Providence at an early day for the purpose of commissioning and mustering the new colored regiments organizing there into the United States service. Several regiments were raised in a short space of time, and officered by men taken from the white troops. The Ninety-fifth furnished a number of commissioned and non-commissioned officers for this purpose, and these colored regiments thus formed were prepared in a few weeks to do important service in the operations which were then going on against Vicksburg.

While the regiment was at Lake Providence the resignation of Colonel L. S. Church was received, and subsequently Lt. Col. Thomas W. Humphrey was advanced to that rank. Since the time Colonel Church was obliged to leave the regiment at Columbus, Kentucky, his health had improved but little, and the prospect of his ever being permitted to rejoin his command became more and more discouraging. Much against his own wishes, and to the universal regret of his officers and men, he resigned his commission in the army. Attended with good health, he must have proven a leading man in the war against the rebellion. Character, talents and influence would have won for him high estimation and rank among military men.

In the month of April, 1863, General Grant assembled his whole army at and near Milliken's Bend, Louisiana, for a grand forward movement across the State, with the intention of striking the Mississippi river at "Hard Times Landing," crossing it near Grand Gulf, and thence around to the rear of Vicksburg.

This was the final experiment originated by him for accomplishing the grand object of the campaign. The attempts to gain a foothold and base of operations up the Yazoo river, and to make the canals at Young's Point and Lake Providence feasible lines of commucation, had been tried and given up, but this last one was destined to be crowned with complete success, and to result in all those glorious consequences which followed in the campaign.

Prior to moving his army by land at this time, the trial of running a number of river transports and gunboats by the numerous batteries which were planted on the bluffs at Vicksburg, was daringly and successfully performed. These steamers were manned by men from different infantry regiments, who volunteered to accompany the boats through the fiery, perilous gauntlet, and who afterward received honorable rewards for their courage and daring, from General Grant and from the Government. The Federal army, which had so long encamped at Lake Providence, commenced embarking on steamers and moving down the river to Milliken's Bend, sixty miles distant, in the latter part of April, 1863, and Colonel Deitzler's brigade, of General McArthur's division, was left at the former place to garrison that post. The Ninety-fifth was subsequently ordered by the division commander from Lake Providence, to take part in the active campaign now opening from Milliken's Bend. It arrived there about the first of May, and the army having moved forward, it immediately pushed on through Richmond, Louisiana, to Smith's Plantation, where General Mc'Arthur's division was then halting. It was here assigned to Brigadier General T. E. G. Ransom's brigade, 6th Division, 17th Army Corps. This brigade was now one of the strongest and best in the whole army, being composed of the Eleventh, Seventy-second and Ninety-fifth Illinois, the Fourteenth and Seventeenth Wisconsin Infantry, and Battery "F," 2nd Illinois Artillery, commanded by Captain J. W. Powell. On the 10th of May the brigade resumed the march, by the way of Perkins' Plantation and Lake St. Joseph, and arrived at "Hard Times Landing" on the 12th. The transports which had successfully passed the batteries at Vicksburg were in readiness at this point to convey the troops across the river to Grand Gulf, and on the same day the regiments of General Ransom's brigade embarked and crossed over to Grand Gulf, which strong rebel position had been recently taken by the advance of General Grant's army. Thus in a few days the whole army of the Tennessee was transferred, by the great military genius directing affairs, to the east side of the

Mississippi, sixty miles below Vicksburg, and was now ready to march rapidly to the rear and to the very gates of that fortress. The line of march from Grand Gulf was by way of Bowl's Creek, Big Sandy and Raymond, where the Ninety-fifth arrived on the 16th of May, the day the great and decisive battle was being fought at Champion Hills and Baker's Creek. General Ransom's brigade pushed forward to take part in the terrible contest there being waged, and arrived on the field just as the Federal army had carried the day and swept everything before it to the Big Black. The regiment took part in the general pursuit which ensued, crossed the Big Black river on the 18th of May, and hurrying on twelve miles farther, camped the same night three-quarters of a mile from the enemy's earth-works in the rear of Vicksburg. The various army corps moved forward with enthusiasm, on different roads, and by sunset of that day the rebel lines around the place were thoroughly invested and all avenues of escape effectually closed. These rapid events necessitated the speedy evacuation by the rebels of Haines' Bluff. The Federal gunboats and transports simultaneously moved up the Yazoo, and here secured a permanent base of supplies, and convenient to the army investing the city.

The following day, May 19th, was to be a busy,

fierce and bloody one for the Army of the Tennessee. A charge was ordered along our whole lines upon the enemy's works, to take place at two o'clock in the afternoon, and at the appointed hour the furious onset commenced. General Sherman's 15th Army Corps occupied the right of the Federal line, resting on the river above Vicksburg; General McPherson's 17th Army Corps held the centre, and the 13th Corps, under General McClernand, held the left, extending nearly to the river on the south side of the city. The ground in front of General Ransom's brigade, and over which it charged at this time, was located near the Jackson road, on the right of the celebrated "White House," and near to the notorious "Fort Hill." Cut, as it was, into deep ravines, and covered with fallen timber, and each ravine being enfiladed by the enemy's fire, it was ground of the very worst character to expose and impede an advancing column. There were intervening ridges to be passed over, which brought the charging regiments into open and close range of a murderous fire of musketry and artillery from the enemy's line.

The Ninety-fifth held an important position in the brigade during this memorable charge, and, led forward by its gallant colonel, advanced under a galling fire to a ridge within one hundred yards of the rebel works, and held the position during the remainder of the day. While maintaining this position Colonel Humphrey received the following dispatch from General Ransom:

"COL.—

You have done *well, nobly.* I desire that you hold your position. Do not expose your men or waste ammunition. I occupy the rear of the ridge back of you. Will move forward as soon as we are supported on the right and left. I expect to hear from General McPherson.

T. E. G. RANSOM,
Brig. Gen'l."

Colonel Humphrey, early in the action, received a wound in the foot, but remained with his command, cheering on his men, until he received orders to withdraw his regiment under cover of darkness that night. Thus the attempt to carry the enemy's works on the 19th, failed at this as well as at all other points on the Federal line, but not without the exhibition of undaunted courage, reckless daring, and the performance of great deeds on the part of our troops. The Ninety-fifth was largely represented in the list of casualties this day, having had seven men killed and fifty-four wounded.

General Grant, with his characteristic perseverance, ordered the assault to be renewed on the 22nd of May, with the intention, if possible, of breaking through the enemy's line at certain points, then of heavily reënforcing the successful assaulting column, with the hope and prospect of thus carrying the day. At ten o'clock A. M., on the 22nd, the charge began again furiously. The Ninety-fifth, on this occasion, also gained an advanced position on the crest of a ridge near the enemy's works, encountering one of the most sweeping and destructive fires to which troops were ever exposed. Colonel Humphrey, in advance of and leading his regiment, exthusiastic with the desire to storm the fortifications in his immediate front, determined to accomplish it, if among human possibilities, and with that natural daring which characterized the man, pressed onward over that ridge, then being swept by rebel musketry, and plowed up by rebel shot and shell. The regiment attempted to follow their leader, and bravely rallied to the charge, but to advance was to meet certain death, and it was plain that a farther prosecution of the undertaking would annihilate the regiment. It had gone into the charge with three hundred and sixty-seven officers and enlisted men in line of battle, and upwards of one hundred of the same had already been rendered hors du combat. Captain Manzer, of Company "C," and Captain Cornwell, of "K," were killed; Major William Avery, Captain Cook, of "D," Lieutenant Smith, of "C," Sponable, of "A," and Pierce, of "I" companies, were severely wounded, while a large percentage of the enlisted men had been killed and wounded. The heroic colonel had gone on in advance, and was given up as killed. Orders came during the afternoon for the murderous and unequal conflict to cease on our part, and the regiment was gradually withdrawn to a neighboring ravine for better protection. Toward night, with thinned ranks, and having left many a gallant soldier killed and wounded on the field, the little band of Ninety-fifth men, exhausted by the efforts of the day, wended its course among the ravines back a short distance to the brigade encampment. The colonel, as has been stated, was supposed to have been killed during the charge, as nothing had been seen or heard of him since he crossed the ridge. General Ransom had ordered a coffin for the reception of the corpse, so certain was he of Colonel Humphrey's death. The latter, however, turned out to be safe, and during the same evening appeared, to the great delight and astonishment of all, at General Ransom's headquarters, where the coffin was then in readiness! After passing over the ridge mentioned, Colonel Humphrey lay down closely upon the ground, as it was impossible for a human being then to be visible above it and live. In this condition, with the mad cannon balls screaming over him, and plowing around his body, covering him with dirt, and benumbing his limbs, he remained until evening, when he noiselessly crept from his precarious position, and appeared so suddenly and unexpectedly in camp, as already related.

Brigadier General Ransom, in his report of these charges, makes the following allusions to the Ninety-fifth :

"On the 19th, the Ninety-fifth Illinois, Colonel Humphrey, commanding, reached a ridge within one hundred yards of the enemy's works, and, though exposed to an enfilading fire of artillery, maintained their position until night, when I withdrew them to a safer position. Early in the action Colonel Humphrey was severely wounded in the foot, but would not leave the field. His loss was much heavier than that of any other regiment in my command.

* * * * * *

"On the 22nd inst., in compliance with the order for a simultaneous assault, at 10 o'clock A. M., I moved my command under cover of my sharp shooters, through a net-work of ravines, filled with fallen timber and cane brake, to a point within sixty yards of the enemy's works, and massed my troops as well as the nature of the ground would admit. Colonel Giles Smith's brigade, of General Sherman's corps, took position at the same time on my right, and the two brigades moved together to the charge. The enemy had, in the meantime, massed troops behind his works in our front, and poured into my ranks one continuous blaze of musketry, while the artillery on my left threw enfilading shot and shell into my columns with deadly effect. Almost at the first fire, two of my leading colonels fell, Colonel Nevins, of the 11th Illinois, killed, and Colonel Humphrey, of the 95th Illinois Infantry, stunned by the concussion of a shell."

The charge of the 22nd of May was, therefore, another failure to accomplish the object desired, and similar results were experienced all along the Federal lines. No portion of the enemy's works had been taken and held, and no point in them was even possessed by our forces at any time during the assault. Great bravery, daring and determination had been everywhere exhibited by the charging columns. They had met with repulse, still they were neither discouraged nor whipped.

Nor was the invincible Grant downcast, or fearful of the consequences. It was only a part of the series of his great attempts by which he finally wrung victory from a stubborn foe. If he failed in one undertaking, he immediately resorted to another; if in that, to a third, and so on, until he accomplished his object. The word *failure* has never been written in his military vocabulary, and the motto, "*Perseverantia vincit omnia*," has carried him wonderfully and steadily forward to the accomplishment of great deeds, and won for him a renown unequaled in history.

After the unsuccessful charges on the 19th and 22nd of May, satisfied that the rebel works could not be carried by assault without great slaughter, General Grant set his whole army at work digging and entrenching, determined to reduce the city by seige. The experience of the past few days had proved it to be in much stronger condition of defense than was anticipated. The necessary delay of the Federal army in crossing the Big Black river, after the battle of Champion Hills, had allowed the enemy, under Pemberton, to collect his forces at Vicksburg, recover partially from recent disaster, and make important preparations on the natural fortifications surrounding the city to receive the advancing Union columns.

The great seige now began, and was prosecuted vigorously; all through the sultry days of May and June, 1863, our lines were gradually advanced toward the enemy's works. Each morning presented some new parallel and newly made forts, from which our artillery could play with nearer and deadlier effect than before.

The regiments of General Ransom's brigade and Captain Powell's artillery, all performed their full share of this long, tedious, but well-rewarded labor, taking important part in constructing the forts, and digging approaches to the enemy's fortifications. By the 3rd of July, the day on which the Confederate garrison surrendered, this brigade had carried its trenches under one of the main forts on the rebel line, and had a mine located there, ready for explosion, when news of the capitulation was announced, and hostilities at once ceased.

On the 4th day of July, 1863, the Ninety-fifth was among the first regiments to enter and take possession of the city. With the victorious stars and stripes unfurled, and with music playing the national airs, these dusty, scarred and war-worn battalions, keeping step to the music of the Union, marched through the streets of Vicksburg, and thence to camps assigned around the city. Soon after the fall of Vicksburg, Port Hudson was surrendered to General Banks, and thus the Mississippi was cleared of rebel obstructions and blockades from Cairo to the Gulf.

On the 12th day of July, General Ransom's brigade was ordered to embark at Vicksburg and proceed to Natchez, for the purpose of occupying that point. It arrived there on the following day, and effected a landing without opposition. The citizens were surprised at this sudden appearance of Federal troops among them, and in a short time after arriving, the place was strongly occupied, and all avenues leading into the city well picketed. Twenty rebel officers and soldiers were captured while attempting to escape. A large Confederate force, under the rebel Colonel Logan, was then stationed in that vicinity to watch the movements of our forces, and to guard the large droves of cattle which were being shipped from Texas through this post, to Johnston's army in the East. It was soon ascertained by General Ransom that a large number of these cattle were then pasturing a few miles east of the city. An expedition was immediately organized of mounted infantry, and started in quest of them. Having advanced about four miles, an immense herd of five thousand Texas cattle was found, and a small rebel guard over them having been put to flight, they were captured, driven back to Natchez, and subsequently shipped to Vicksburg. Information was also received that within a few days one hundred and fifty wagons loaded with ordnance stores for Kirby Smith, had been ferried across at Natchez to the Louisiana shore. Another force of mounted infantry accordingly was sent in pursuit, overtook the train fifteen miles out, captured the rear-guard, consisting of a lieutenant and a few men, and brought back three hundred and twelve new Austrian muskets, two hundred and three thousand rounds of cartridges, eleven boxes of artillery ammunition, and destroyed a large quantity of ammunition which could not be moved. This force of mounted infantry was made up from the several regiments of the brigade, using such spare horses as were found in the vicinity, and all placed under command of Major Asa Worden, of the 14th Wisconsin Infantry. That portion of it which represented the Ninety-fifth was in charge of Captain Charles B. Loop. There being no regular cavalry furnished General Ransom at this place, he was obliged to organize a band of this kind for scouting and other purposes around Natchez, and on many occasions it rendered the Government very efficient service. On the 22nd of July, Major Worden's mounted command (two hundred strong,) started from Natchez on a two days' scout in the country east of the city, making a circuit through Washington, Woodville and Kingston. During this scout the party destroyed two hundred and seven thousand rounds of infantry ammunition, found concealed in a ravine, and fifty-six boxes of artillery ammunition. They also found large quantities of "C. S. A." cotton.

On the 26th, it was again sent out in the direction

of the Mississippi Central Railroad, with orders to reconnoitre the country, seize and destroy or secure any ammunition or other supplies for the rebel army, mount and remount his men from horses picked up in the country, and to destroy the railroad and telegraph communication with Mobile as fully as practicable. The expedition on this trip consisted of three hundred and fifty mounted men and one piece of artillery, and made a march of about one hundred and thirty miles, passing through Kingston, Liberty and Woodville. At Liberty seventeen hogsheads of sugar, one hundred and fifty saddles, one artillery carriage, one government wagon and fifty stands of small arms were destroyed. At Woodville Major Worden struck the railroad, consigned to the flames a large cotton factory containing forty looms, used in the manufacturing of cloth for the rebel army, fourteen freight and two passenger cars, destroyed two railroad locomotives, two hundred and fifty barrels of C. S. A. molasses, a large amount of army clothing, and captured and brought back to Natchez one rebel lieutenant and nine enlisted men; also a six-pounder gun of French manufacture, said to have been used by General Jackson at New Orleans.

On the 30th of July information was received by General Ransom, through scouts and negroes and others, that the rebel Logan, with a mounted force of about fifteen hundred strong, was moving on Natchez, and would strike at that point the following morning. Every preparation was, therefore, made to receive them. At about sunrise on the 31st the rebels were discovered approaching in force on the Washington road. General Ransom's pickets had been strengthened sufficiently to check their advance; Major Worden was immediately dispatched with his mounted men to reconnoitre the enemy's flanks, parties of videttes were sent out on all the roads, and a regiment of infantry and a section of artillery were ordered to the support of the cavalry. Skirmishing now commenced briskly, and the rebels fell back at our approach. Major Worden and his mounted men continued to drive them slowly, keeping up a desultory fight until noon, when the enemy made a stand and formed a line of battle on a rise of ground about eleven miles out from the city. The Major's force, which had left the infantry near Natchez, being two small to attack the enemy in his position, and discovering an attempt being made to turn his flank, he fell back half a mile, where he met and attacked a party of one hundred men who had been sent to his rear. These he routed, and took one lieutenant and sixteen men prisoners. He then fell back three miles farther, took good position, and waited several hours for an attack. No farther demonstrations being made by the enemy, the mounted infantry was withdrawn, and soon afterward returned to the city. In this affair Logan lost his chief of cavalry, Colonel Powers, fifteen men wounded, and forty-five prisoners. The Federals did not lose a man, and had only two slightly wounded.

General Ransom, during his administration at Natchez, greatly felt the need of more cavalry with which he might pursue and fight Logan. The temporary mounted force organized from the infantry, was inadequate to meet the larger force of Logan, though it always rendered a good account of itself. The general applied repeatedly to the head-quarters at Vicksburg for a reënforcement of cavalry, but for some reason it was never furnished him. To use his own words, in a report to Lieut. Col. Wm. T. Clark, Asst. Adjt. General of the 17th Army Corps, "It is a terrible annoyance to have this vagabond (Logan) so near me, and not be able to fight him."

The brigade remained at Natchez until the middle of October following, busily employed in attending to the rebel bands infesting that vicinity, collecting the large quantities of Confederate States cotton found in the neighborhood, and preserving good order and restoring confidence among the people. Large numbers of negroes, on the arrival and during the stay of the brigade here, flocked into the camps to receive protection and their freedom under the emancipation proclamation. So great was the rush made by this released element of population, that the general commanding was obliged to establish a corral for them outside the city, and furnish them with rations provided by the Government. The citizens of the place became alarmed at the consequences which might follow from the sudden liberation of the race which had hitherto been held in subjection by them, and appealed to General Ransom for protection against anticipated but groundless dangers from this source. Numerous planters sent in applications for the negroes to be set at work again with their former masters, and gather the crops then maturing. The general replied to such, that the design of the army was solely to crush out of existence an armed rebellion, and reëstablish the supremacy of the government of the United States; that except in so far as it was necessary for this purpose, private property would not be molested, unless a disposition was manifested to use it for the benefit of the armies we were fighting; that it was his wish to encourage, by all the means in his power, the peaceful avocations of the people, to have the laboring classes remain on the plantations, and cultivate and harvest the growing crops; and that while he was in duty bound to recognize and encourage the freedom of the negroes, every inducement would be held out for them to remain where they were and work for reasonable wages. The negro question at all times during the progress of the war, was an annoying subject to military commanders, in endeavoring to carry out the policy of the Government in reference to this matter. General Ransom found it so in his management of affairs at Natchez. The line of duty and right was plainly marked out, however. The freedom of the negro had been plainly and firmly decreed months since by the President, backed up by the Congress and the loyal people of the United States. It was too late for the importunities of rebels now professing devotion to the Union, to avail anything toward reclaiming to bondage those unfortunate beings, in whom they had forfeited every right, title and interest, and who, according to all the rights of war, as well as of humanity, were as free as those who sought to reënslave them. Gradually the planters around Natchez became reconciled to the altered condition of labor in their midst, employed the negroes as freedmen toiling for compensation, and accepted the new policy inaugurated by the commanding officer, as a consequence of that rebellion which, until quite recently, they had ardently supported.

Large numbers of negroes were here furnished for the various regiments of colored troops which at this time were being raised at Vicksburg and other points. In this manner their accumulation on the hands of the military commander was in a measure avoided, and the freedmen were made of important use to the Government.

While the Ninety-fifth was in camp at Natchez, General McArthur, commanding the division, paid a visit to his troops at this post, and, on invitation from Colonel Humphrey, attended a dress parade of this regiment. The colonel had duly prepared his men for such exhibition, and by constant drill had trained them to proficiency in this beautiful military exercise. He caused the colors to be escorted to and from the parade ground strictly in accordance with the tactics, a part which other regiments seldom performed, but which always adds interest to the parade, and shows a due respect and protection for the flag of the Union — ever to be defended and never surrendered. The general expressed himself greatly pleased with the appearance of the regiment, and he and his staff joined in the opinion that they had never witnessed a more perfect dress parade during the service.

A Natchez many of the officers and enlisted men obtained leave of absence and furloughs, and improved the opportunity of visiting their homes in the North. After the surrender of Vicksburg, General Grant decided, with great liberality and kindness, that these favors should be extensively granted to the troops who had followed him through the recent campaigns' which they had helped him crown with success. As there was to be no farther general campaign in the Southwest during the fall, most of the soldiers could enjoy these privileges of visiting home without detriment to the service.

About the middle of October, 1863, the brigade, (now commanded by Brigadier General Thomas K. Smith,) was ordered from Natchez to Vicksburg. The regiment remained at the latter place during the fall and winter, assisting in constructing the Federal fortifications around the city, and performing garrison, picket and other duties. It had now been in the service a little over one year, and had become greatly reduced in numbers by deaths in battle and from disease, discharges, and transfers to other commands. The President, during the same fall, called for three hundred thousand more men to fill up the depleted ranks in the field, and recruiting parties were sent North by the different regiments for this purpose.

Early in November, 1863, Captain C. B. Loop, of Company "B," Captain James Nish, of Company "I," and Captain A. S. Stewart, of Company "A," accompanied by several non-commissioned officers, were detailed to proceed North and obtain recruits for the Ninety-fifth. They forwarded a large number to the regiment during the same winter, filling it to more than a minimum number.

CHAPTER V.

Expeditions from Vicksburg in Spring of 1864 — Sherman's March to Meridian — Colonel Coates' defense of Yazoo City — The Red River Expedition — Taking of Fort DeRussey — Ninety-fifth detailed to destroy the works — Arrival at Alexandria — March to Grand Ecore — Ascending the River on Transports — Battle of Pleasant Hill — Retreat ordered by General Banks — Return of the Fleet — Running Batteries at Vandares — Ninety-fifth as Rear Guard of Banks' Army — Two Days' Fight at Clouterville — Retreat to Alexandria — Battle of Yellow Bayou — Evacuation of the Red River Country — Return of the Ninety-fifth to Vicksburg.

EARLY in the spring of 1864, several expeditions were organized at Vicksburg for the purpose of visiting certain interior sections of the Confederacy, where the Federal arms had not yet penetrated, where rebellion was yet defiant, and from whence it continued to receive important means of support. The first of these was organized by General Sherman, and set out from Vicksburg in the fore part of February, in the direction of Montgomery, Alabama. It consisted of the 16th Army Corps, under Major General Hurlbut, and the 17th, commanded by Major General McPherson. Crossing the Big Black river at the bridge, this force swept on toward Jackson, the two corps taking different roads. The enemy were found in position three miles out from Jackson, and were attacked and routed by the advancing Federal columns. The army crossed Pearl river upon pontoons, and advanced rapidly as far east as Meridian, Mississippi, where important railroad communications, arsenals and Confederate stores were successfully destroyed.

This expedition was absent about twenty days, and having accomplished its objects, returned to Vicksburg in the latter part of February.

General Sherman, prior to leaving Vicksburg on the Meridian "raid," sent Colonel James H. Coates with the Eleventh Illinois, a colored regiment, and a small force of cavalry, up the Yazoo valley, with orders to proceed cautiously and attract the attention of a force of rebel cavalry known to be in that vicinity watching the movements going on at Vicksburg. This cavalry was under Ross and Richardson, and they intended to make a dash upon the lengthy wagon train of General Sherman's army. It was Colonel Coates' mission to divert their attention, and prevent the consummation of their object. Ascending the Yazoo with his small command, to Sartatia, he here encountered the enemy in force, immediately landed his troops and gave battle. Aided by the gunboat which accompanied the expedition, the enemy was quickly driven back and put to flight.

The troops then reëmbarked upon the transports and proceeded up the river to Yazoo City without farther molestation. Colonel Coates had orders to continue his expedition as far as Greenville, some miles above on the river, in case the enemy did not appear in too strong force. He arrived there without serious interruption, and afterward completely destroyed the works of Fort Pemberton, a strong position at the confluence of the Tallahatchie and Yazoo rivers. He subsequently returned down the river to Yazoo City, collected a large quantity of Confederate cotton in this vicinity, and forwarded the same to the proper authorities at Vicksburg. On the 6th day of March, while at this post, he was attacked by the mounted forces under Generals Ross and Richardson, consisting of seven regiments, and numbering three or four thousand strong. The rebels dashed in suddenly on the Benton road, and attempted to take the place by surprise. Colonel Coates having disposed his small force to receive them warmly, determined to hold the place at all hazards. A portion of the Eleventh Illinois, commanded by Major McKee, occupied the fort on the hill near the Benton road, upon which the enemy charged repeatedly, but each time were repulsed with great slaughter. The fighting became general all around and in the city, and raged furiously through the principal streets. For a time it seemed as if the superior forces of the enemy, as they swarmed in from all points, would capture the entire garrison, and, indeed, a report of that nature *was* carried to Major General McPherson, at Vicksburg. But it turned out otherwise. General Ross forwarded, under flag of truce, a note to Colonel Coates, stating that the latter could not expect to hold out against such superior odds, and asked him to surrender, and spare farther effusion of blood. Coates sent word back that he had no idea of capitulating, and that he intended to hold the place till the last. One of the rebel commanders sent a dispatch to Major McKee, in command at the fort, asking him to surrender, and that in case he refused, no quarter would be granted him. McKee, fired to anger by the insulting request, made the following characteristic reply: "I don't *scare* worth a *damn*. We are ready for you."

The fight was continued with desperation on both sides all day long, until finally the Confederates gave up the contest, and leaving behind a large number of killed and wounded, retreated on the road toward

Benton. The Federal loss was quite light, considering the forces engaged. Of course, in the exhausted condition of his troops, Colonel Coates was unable to pursue the enemy, and contented himself with what had been accomplished during the day. He soon afterward received orders to return to Vicksburg with his command, and arrived there about the time the Red river expedition was setting out.

I have been thus particular in giving an account of this successful expedition, because it was principally performed by the Eleventh Illinois, with which the Ninety-fifth was then brigaded, and had been intimately and pleasantly associated since entering the service. As auxiliary to the main operations of General Sherman at that time, it may be said to have been really the only brilliant affair that occurred during the whole movement. In its management, Colonel Coates had proven himself a brave and efficient officer, and every way worthy to command in times of emergency. By his gallant conduct and meritorious service at Yazoo City, he was well entitled to a star from the hands of the Government. Through a sensitive modesty, however, which prevented him from pushing his claims, this was not accorded him until long afterward, near the close of the rebellion, when he was brevetted a brigadier general. The Ninety-fifth did not accompany these expeditions, as the brigade to which it was attached, with the exception of the Eleventh Illinois, received orders to remain and garrison Vicksburg during the absence of the main army. At this time the brigade was commanded by Colonel Malloy, of the 17th Wisconsin. Shortly after these events, an expedition in aid of a similar one, preparing under General Banks, at New Orleans, for the purpose of ascending the Red river, was organized at Vicksburg. Forces were selected for this object from the 16th and 17th Army Corps, two divisions being detached from the former, and one, under command of Brigadier Thomas Kilby Smith, from the latter. The whole force, from both corps, had for its commander then Brigadier General A. J. Smith.

The Ninety-fifth was temporarily detached from the 2nd Brigade, 17th Army Corps, and assigned to a brigade made up for the Red River expedition, consisting of the 14th Wisconsin, 81st and 95th Illinois, and commanded by Colonel L. M. Ward. These troops, thus organized, embarked at Vicksburg on the 9th day of March, 1865. The Ninety-fifth went aboard the steamer "John Raines," and on the tenth the whole command moved down the river, arriving at the mouth of Red river on the 11th. The army under General Banks had not yet arrived from New

Orleans, and General Smith, on the 12th, proceeded up Red river with his own force.

Having ascended twenty miles, a landing was made at Simsport, near Atchfalaya Pass, and the Ninety-fifth took part in the skirmish which ensued at that place, driving back the enemy. The march was commenced from this place at 9 o'clock P. M., on the evening of the 13th, and continued until 3 A. M., the following morning, in the direction of Fort DeRussey, where General Smith's force arrived on the 14th, attacked and captured the stronghold, and took three hundred prisoners. On the 16th, the Ninety-fifth was assigned the task of destroying the well-constructed fortifications at this place, and under the especial superintendence of Colonel Humphrey the work was rapidly and effectually performed. The following is an extract from Colonel Humphrey's report in reference to the same :

"The works were very formidable, being by far the most scientifically and permanently constructed works of the enemy I have seen, and with our limited appliances, very difficult of destruction. The interior slope of the main redoubt, covering an area of about ten thousand five hundred square yards, was wholly revetted with heavy (fourteen inch) square timber, firmly pinned upon each other, morticed and tenanted at the angles. These, with great labor, were wedged off one by one, pulled down with ropes, and piled for burning. All this was accomplished at 5 o'clock P. M., (16th inst.), and as my orders were to burn nothing until farther orders, I complimented my command for the zeal with which they had worked, and the success of their labor, and marched them back to the brigade camp, distant only about one hundred and fifty yards from the fort.

"At seven o'clock P. M., I was notified that the magazines, (three of them within the main redoubt), one of them containing about fifty kegs and barrels of powder, would be exploded at eight o'clock. I was ordered to embark my transportation, and immediately after the explosion, to burn the timber I had previously prepared for that purpose, and be ready to embark my men at an early hour. I received no orders to move my command to a place of greater safety, and did not feel at liberty to leave my position in the brigade without farther orders. My company commanders were notified of the danger, and the men fell back from one to two hundred yards, availing themselves of such protection as they could find. One and two hours passed beyond the appointed time, and the explosion did not take place. The night was cold, and the men weary from their day's work; one by one, many of them resought their bunks and bivouac fires, when, at about half past ten o'clock, the magazines blew up with a terrific explosion, sinking the earth beneath one's feet, and filling the air, for hundreds of yards, with timbers, huge lumps of hard, red clay, and other dangerous missiles. Samuel Snyder, of Company "A," had his left leg broken by a lump of clay, so as to require amputation above the knee, and is not expected to live. Lieutenant John D. Abbe, Company "K," was slightly wounded in the face,— also several others, while many narrowly escaped death. Soon after the explosion of the magazine, an iron field-piece, situated in the west part of the fort, bursted, scattering fragments of the gun through the brigade camp, killing, among others in the brigade, private Samuel Jackson, Company "C," of my regiment.

"About twelve o'clock P. M., I proceeded to burn the piled timbers, which left the fortifications in ruins, and as thoroughly destroyed as possible within such a limited time."

On the 17th day of March the regiment reëmbarked at Gordon's Landing, near the fort, and proceeded up the river, sixty miles, arriving at Alexandria the same evening. On the 18th, it disembarked at Pineville, on the right hand side of the river, and marched out twelve miles on a foraging expedition, returning the same day. On the 25th, Companies "G" and "D," of the Ninety-fifth, were detailed as guard over prisoners, and started with them the same day for New Orleans, on the steamer "Meteor." The Thirteenth Army Corps, commanded by General Franklin, having now arrived at Alexandria, from below, the whole army, provided with three days' rations, moved forward on the 26th, along Bayou Rupee, and on the following day arrived at Bayou Cotille, where the regiment remained until April 1st. Companies "G" and "D" having delivered their prisoners to the authorities at New Orleans, returned to this place and rejoined the regiment.

On the 4th of April the army reached Grand Ecore, and from here the 13th and 19th corps, and a large portion of General A. J. Smith's command, immediately marched up the river in the direction of Shreveport, to meet the enemy, while the division of the 17th Army Corps, under General Kilby Smith, ascended the river on transports, loaded with supplies for General Banks' army.

Prior to the general movement of the boats, at this time, the Ninety-fifth was sent on a scouting expedition a few miles up the river, a small force of rebels holding position on the shore being reported in the vicinity.

Embarking on the steamer "Universe," it moved up to a small town by the name of Campte, arriving about noon, April 5th. The regiment here disembarked, and, provided with one day's rations in haversacks, marched into the country. After advancing two or three miles, information was received that the enemy had retreated, and the troops then countermarched to the steamer, and soon rejoined the fleet lying near Grand Ecore. On the 8th of April, the whole fleet of transports commenced moving up the river from Grand Ecore, to coöperate with the land forces. The Ninety-fifth was arranged on the various steamers as follows: Companies "B," "E," "G," "H," "I" and "K," occupied the "Sioux City," and Companies "B" and "G," were detailed as sharpshooters. Company "A" was placed as guard on the "Black Hawk," General Banks' head-quarters boat; "F" on the "Hastings," General Kilby Smith's head-quarters; "C" on the "Meteor," and "D" on the "Shreveport." The fleet had ascended some seventy miles above Grand Ecore without much hindrance, except occasional firing from the river banks, when, on the 10th, intelligence was brought through by an orderly that General Banks' army had been defeated at "Pleasant Hill," and was then retreating on Grand Ecore. A speedy return of the fleet down the river was ordered, and was necessary for its salvation. Already the rebels had erected batteries below, with the design of entrapping the returning transports, and on the 12th and 13th of April, the Ninety-fifth took active part in successively passing them, under a heavy fire of artillery and musketry. Colonel Humphrey, in his report of that portion of the expedition, says: "On April thirteenth, at one o'clock P. M., I ran a gauntlet of a four-gun battery (12 pounders,) well posted, and musketry. The shots were fired at the pilot-house 'Sioux City,' with great precision, the first grazing the hurricane deck just forward of the pilot-house, demolishing at that point my breastworks of hard bread, wounding slightly First Sergeant William Andrews, of Company 'E,' and another soldier. The balance of the shells missed the pilot-house but a few feet, and exploded with great precision. I had taken the precaution to fortify my decks as much as possible with hay, hard bread, and every available article, so that my men were quite well protected from musketry, to which precaution, and the admirable coolness with which my sharpshooters played upon the enemy, I attribute, in a great measure, my escape with so little loss."

The regiment reached Grand Ecore on the 14th and 15th of April, having had one killed and eleven wounded on the passage down. It remained here in camp until the 20th, when the retreat was resumed by the army, the Ninety-fifth forming the rearguard, and expecting an attack at any moment by the pursuing enemy, now flushed and emboldened by his recent successes. The line of retreat was on the Nachitoches road. On the 22nd, a few hours after leaving the city of Nachitoches, three thousand rebels attacked the rear of General Banks' army, then guarded by Colonel Ward's brigade. The Ninety-fifth being the rear regiment, was the first to form in line of battle and receive the attack. An hour's fight ensued, in which the enemy was driven back in confusion. In this engagement, Sergeant Caleb Cornwell, of Company "K," was killed by a ball passing through his head, and he was buried on the following day at Clouterville. Near this place, on the 23rd, while the Ninety-fifth still held the rear, the rebels again came up and opened with three pieces of artillery. Colonel Ward's entire brigade immediately formed in line of battle, and engaged in a furious conflict which lasted two hours. Here, too, the rebels were handsomely repulsed. On the same day the Federal army was attacked in front, resulting in complete defeat to the enemy. At night the regiment bivouacked, after a short march, and at an early hour on the following morning the Union camps were aroused by the enemy's shells from the rear. In this action the Ninety-fifth took an important part, and the attacking force was driven back with heavy loss. The army arrived at Alexandria on the 28th of April, having been constantly harassed by the enemy.

At this place a halt was made for several days, while the gunboats and transports could be passed below the falls. Since the army had been absent on the expedition, the river had fallen so much that it became necessary to build a dam and float the boats over this difficult place in the river. Meanwhile the enemy was active, and threatening attack on every side, but our land forces were so disposed as to hold them in check until the safety of the steamers could be secured. The Ninety-fifth, with other troops, was sent out to Governor More's plantation, and remained there several days, watching the movements of the enemy, and preventing his advance.

By the 14th day of May the gunboats and transports had successfully passed over the falls. Alexandria was evacuated, a large quantity of cotton, which cotton speculators had gathered in there, was burned, including a portion of the city itself, and the whole army again resumed the retreat. On the 15th, at dark, the Ninety-fifth arrived at Fort DeRussey, and passed on fifteen miles farther. Sharp skirmishing took place at Marksville, and an important artillery duel occurred at Mansouri, in which the rebels were badly worsted. On the 16th, the enemy offered battle in front, and as usual, was repulsed, and on the 17th he was again defeated in an attack on the rear of the Federal army, then held by General Mower's division, of the 16th Army Corps. On the 18th, occurred the hard-fought battle of Yellow Bayou, in which the rebels fought desperately, but were everywhere overwhelmed with defeat, losing three hundred prisoners and many killed and wounded. The 16th corps was hotly engaged, and the Ninety-fifth fought during a portion of the time under one of the severest fires of artillery it ever experienced in a field fight. Fortunately, however, the regiment was so near to the enemy's batteries that most of their shot and shell passed over the men without injuring them. The Federal loss was heavy, and several of the regiments (among them the 58th Illinois,) were badly cut to pieces. After this severe contest, in which the enemy was well punished, the forces under General Banks met with no farther hindrance of importance, in evacuating the country, and reached the mouth of Red river on the 21st day of May, 1864.

Thus ended, ingloriously, the great, expensive and fruitless attempt to penetrate to the head-waters of the

Red river. Not inglorious for the troops composing the expedition, for they at all times performed their whole duty, and even after the battle of Pleasant Hill, stood ready to fight their way to Shreveport, and would certainly have done so, had they been commanded to that effect, and led in that direction. General A. J. Smith, the brave leader of the 16th Army Corps, confident of whipping the enemy and reaching Shreveport, desired not to give up the contest in that manner; but the disheartened commanding officer of the army, supposing his forces had met with great defeat, and fearing they would be annihilated by a farther prosecution of his undertaking, decided to abandon the expedition, and ordered the long and tedious retreat to the Mississippi. It is a well-known fact that both armies, supposing themselves defeated, retreated about the same time, and equal distances from the battle field of Pleasant Hill, and on the following day, each party sent in flags of truce for the purpose of burying their dead — each expecting to find the other occupying and holding the ground where the battle had raged. It was in truth no more a defeat for the Federals than the rebels, and it was a general belief in the army that a few more days of perseverance would have placed the great object of the expedition in possession of the Union troops. The order to retreat was imperative, however, but was obeyed with feelings of reluctance and disappointment.

On the 22nd of April, the Ninety-fifth embarked at the mouth of the Red river upon the steamer "Golden Era," sailed up the Mississippi, and reached Vicksburg on the 23rd. When the regiment left this place, in March previous, it was well understood and so expressed in the orders, that it was only temporarily detached from the 17th Army Corps, then encamped there, and after the completion of the Red River expedition, which was originally intended to take twenty days, it was expected to rejoin the command at Vicksburg, where it properly belonged. The most of that corps had, meanwhile, been ordered up the river to Cairo, and had moved forward to take part in the Georgia campaign, then about opening. The detachment, camp and garrison equipage and baggage of the Ninety-fifth, which had been left at Vicksburg, was also taken in the same direction, though it was known that the regiment was to return soon to that place. The brigade to which it legitimately belonged was still at Vicksburg on its arrival, but it was no longer considered as belonging to the command from which it had been loaned for the time being, and for some reason, through orders never explained, it was sent to Memphis, Tenn.

CHAPTER VI.

Arrival of the Regiment at Memphis — Assigned to General Sturgis' Expedition — March from Memphis — Battle of Guntown, Miss. — Colonel Humphrey killed — Captain Stewart takes command, and is severely wounded — Death of Captain Bush — Command taken by Captain Schellenger — The Regiment fight with desperation — Ammunition giving out — Absence of Commanding Officers — Ninety-fifth fall back, after a long conflict against superior odds — Form second line of battle — Final Retreat on Memphis — Hardships — Arrival of the Regiment back to Memphis in deplorable condition — Comments on the Guntown affair.

THE regiment arrived at Memphis in the latter part of May, 1864, just in time to be assigned to the ill-fated and disastrous expedition under General Sturgis, which, early in June, set out from that point to meet the rebel General Forrest, who was then operating extensively in Northern Mississippi. The Ninety-fifth was placed in a brigade with the 81st and 113th Illinois Infantry, and the troops left Memphis June 1st, taking the cars on the Memphis and Charleston railroad, to the twenty-sixth mile post, where they camped the same night. The line of march was afterward through Lafayette, Lamar Station, on the Mississippi Central Railroad, Salem, Miss., and Ripley, where the expedition arrived on the 9th. The weather was excessively hot, and rapid marching beneath such a sun ill prepared the men for a sudden fight. On the 10th, Sturgis' cavalry had advanced several miles ahead of his infantry column, and brought on an engagement before they could be easily supported. Word soon came back to the infantry, then five or six miles distant, to advance on the double-quick and support the cavalry. Colonel Humphrey, knowing that his men were already greatly fatigued, and desiring to bring them into action in as good and efficient condition as possible, would not double-quick his command, but pressed forward on a quick march. The regiment hastened on to the scene of conflict, now raging furiously at the front; numbers of the men, overcome by heat and fatigue, fell out by the roadside, while the large majority of them, though well nigh exhausted, and unfit to perform what, under better circumstances they would have accomplished, even in the unequal contest before them, still held their position in the ranks, and came up bravely to form their first line of battle.

The battle occurred near Guntown, Mississippi, and the position of the Ninety-fifth in the line formed was an important one, and was held obstinately for a long time by the regiment. In the early part of the action, Colonel Humphrey, while leading on his men, fell, mortally wounded, and the command devolved upon Captain Wm. H. Stewart, Company "F," next in rank present. He had charge but a short time before receiving a severe wound through both thighs, and was carried helpless from the field. Captain E. N. Bush, of Company "G," then assumed command, and shortly he, too, was stricken down and counted among the fallen and killed. Then Captain Schellenger, of Company "K," was called to the command of the gallant band, and though their brave colonel and other commanders had fallen, one after another, yet the fight was continued with indescribable desperation. Meanwhile the enlisted men, as well as officers, were falling thick and fast from right to left of the regimental line; the ammunition was fast giving out, and none arrived from the rear to replete the empty cartridge-boxes. Neither the commanding officer of the troops, nor staff officers, appeared at the front, directing movements or bringing reënforcements to assist and strengthen the faltering Federal lines. They were not there to encourage or to share in the terrible fatalities of that eventful day. The enemy was, meanwhile, being reënforced, and with deadly volleys sorely pressed and harassed the unsupported and now trembling Union ranks, which for hours had stood boldly facing the leaden shower and fierce artillery. Finally, both flanks of the regiment were turned by overpowering numbers of the enemy, and it was obliged to fall back, or suffer entire capture. Determined, however, not to give up the contest until the last moment, it took position again near some artillery a short distance in the rear, here formed its second line of battle, and withstood for a time the vigorous assaults of the rebels, now advancing rapidly, and flushed with the certainty of victory. Soon afterward a general and hasty retreat was ordered by Sturgis, and his whole army, infantry, cavalry and artillery, fled precipitately in the direction of Memphis; he and a large portion of his cavalry being far in advance of all, leaving the scattered organizations of infantry and artillery to effect their escape in the best way they could.

The enemy, victorious at all points, lost no time in pursuit of the routed and demoralized Union troops, pressing them vigorously on all sides, capturing a large amount of our artillery, and taking many of the disorganized army prisoners. The remnant of the Ninety-fifth was led back to Memphis by Captain Schellenger, but amid the excitement and confusion which prevailed, a return as a regimental organization was impossible, and each man looked out particularly for himself. Great credit is due to Captain Schellenger for the able manner in which he conducted the retreat. On the 11th, 12th and 13th days of June, and the nights of those days, the surviving and uncaptured men of the regiment made lengthy and rapid strides toward the city of Memphis, and evaded successfully the vigilance and grasp of the pursuers. When the knapsack became too onerous, the men unslung and abandoned it, and around many a tree did they bend and break their faithful guns, to prevent capture both of themselves and fire arms by the enemy. Finally, on the 13th, the fragment of the regiment, under Captain Schellenger, worn out and nearly famished, succeeded in reaching Memphis. For days afterward, however, a few kept straggling in, all in most deplorable condition.

Colonel Humphrey's body was brought off from the field while the fight was progressing, and Surgeon Green succeeded in bringing it through to Memphis in a buggy obtained at Salem. That of Captain E. N. Bush was not found, and remained on the field, together with the most of those who fell during the engagement. The regiment had never before experienced such disaster as had recently overwhelmed it. Their gallant leader had been taken away, many valuable officers and men had been killed, wounded and taken prisoners, and the consequent demoralization was necessarily so great that the organization became for a time well nigh annihilated.

The battle of Guntown, and the defeat, rout and subsequent flight of the Federal army, will stand forth in the history of the rebellion as one of the most shameful exhibitions of generalship on record. Bravery on the part of our troops was not wanting, nor were they in any manner to blame for the failure. They were veterans who had participated in the memorable charges on the 19th and 22nd of May, 1862, at Vicksburg, in the long seige which ensued, and in the various battles fought during the Red River expedition. They had never before known defeat, under some of the most trying circumstances experienced during the whole war. The true cause of the great misfortune was plainly *incompetency* and *lack of courage* on the part of one who should have been the leading spirit of the occasion. When the important crisis of battle came, which demanded his counsel, presence and action, he was nowhere to be found near the front, where the fierce contest raged, and for a time fluctuated with doubtful signs of success to either side. Without orders, and without the means of prosecuting the fight, the valiant troops held out until the last moment, and fell back only when impending ruin was about to overwhelm the Union army. They performed their whole duty, and could not accomplish impossibilities.

After the return of the regiment to Memphis, the remains of Colonel Humphrey were taken North to his family, where appropriate funeral services were held, under the direction of the Masonic Order. A very large concourse of people assembled from the surrounding country, and attended the corpse to the burial place selected for its reception, near his prairie home. Beneath the green sod of his own beautiful homestead, under the cool shades of the tall walnut trees he so much admired, and near to the wife and children of his heart, they laid away in peaceful repose the remains of the gallant, noble and beloved colonel. Those who associated with him in camp, on the march, and in battle, and in all the various and arduous duties of soldier-life, are best acquainted with the military ability, the unremitting zeal, the integrity of character, the urbanity of manners, and the nobility of soul, which ever characterized the man. Yet his immediate associates are not the only ones who know this, for among the numerous officers, both of superior and inferior rank, belonging to the various commands with which his regiment was identified in the field, he was held in the highest respect and estimation, his bravery universally acknowledged and lauded, and everywhere throughout the army, where he was known, he was mentioned as one of the most brave, industrious, persevering and promising military men which the country had afforded. By the survivors of that regiment which he so long, so faithfully, and so honorably commanded, his valor, his virtues, his overflowing kindness of heart, and his constant solicitude for their comfort and welfare, under some of the most disadvantageous circumstances, will always be deeply cherished in memory, and the prairie burial spot which contains his sacred ashes, will ever be approached with reverence, and regarded as the resting place of a brave soldier, a true patriot, and an estimable citizen.

CHAPTER VII.

The Regiment relieved from duty for a time after the Guntown Battle, and allowed to recruit — The Command soon regains a prosperous condition, and prepares for the Arkansas Expedition, under General Mower — Arrival at St. Charles, Ark. — Company "K" detached and left at the mouth of White River as Garrison — Regiment ascends White River to Duvall's Bluff, and goes by Railroad to Brownsville — The lengthy March through Arkansas to Missouri in search of Price — Arrival at Camp Girardeau — "Colonel Pap," and why he was so named — Regiment embarks for St. Louis, and goes to Jefferson City — Ordered forward to Sedalia — Assigned to Garrison Duty — Remain there until the Campaign against Price closes — General A. J. Smith's troops sent to Benton Barracks, St. Louis.

ON the return of the regiment from Guntown to Memphis, its organization had been so much shattered by recent misfortunes that it was relieved for a time from the performance of other than light duties, and was allowed a few weeks to recover from the severe shock it had received, before taking part in an expedition which was soon to set out from Memphis for Arkansas, under command of General Mower.

On the 20th of July, Major William Avery, who had been absent on recruiting service in Illinois, and had been serving on court martial at Springfield, Ill., for a long time, returned to the regiment and assumed command, and on the 26th of the same month, Lieut. Colonel L. Blanden, who, soon after the Red River expedition, was ordered North on business, rejoined the regiment at Memphis. The regiment now underwent a thorough course of reparation and discipline. New arms and clothing replaced the old ones lost and destroyed during the Guntown expedition, and soon the command, by constant drilling and unremitting efforts on the part of the officers and men, regained its former condition of prosperity and efficiency, and was pronounced well prepared in every way to reënter upon active duties in the field.

Preparations were now being made for the movement of troops down the Mississippi and up the White river, for the purpose of operating in Arkansas. On the 3rd of August, 1864, the Ninety-fifth embarked on the steamer "White Cloud," at Memphis, and arrived at St. Charles, Arkansas, on the 5th. Company "K" was detached from the regiment at the mouth of White river, and assigned to garrison that post. The division of the 17th Army Corps commanded by Colonel J. B. Moore, to which the Ninety-fifth belonged, remained at St. Charles until September 1st, building fortifications and performing picket duty. For several mornings in succession the regiments lay in line of battle, expecting an attack from the enemy, but none occurred. Little Rock was at this time threatened by the enemy under the rebel General Price, and yet it was uncertain exactly where that cunning Confederate leader intended to strike, whether he would attempt to seize Little Rock, where Major General Steele then commanded, or make one of his annual raids into the State of Missouri. A portion of the troops belonging to the 16th Army Corps, under Major General A. J. Smith, had gone up the river from Memphis, and landed in Missouri, to operate against Price if he should come that way, while another portion of his command, in charge of General Mower, was concentrating at Brownsville, on the railroad between Duvall's Bluff and Little Rock, and within easy supporting distance of the latter place. The Ninety-fifth left the post of St. Charles, September 1st, and proceeded with Colonel Moore's division up White river to Duvall's Bluffs. From here these troops were ordered farther up the river, to meet a rebel force reported in that vicinity. A sharp skirmish took place near Augusta, in which the enemy met with severe loss. There was but a small force of rebels found, however, and they, after slight resistance, fled at the approach of our troops.

The regiment returned down the river Sept. 6th, to Duvall's Bluff, and on the following day was ordered to proceed by railroad from that place to Brownsville, where it arrived the same night, and bivouacked by the cars. It was about this time that the real intentions of Price were made known, and it became certain that he was invading the State of Missouri with a large force. As soon as this was ascertained, General Mower immediately prepared his command of nearly ten thousand men, then collected at Brownsville, for an active campaign; put them in light marching order, and on the 17th of September pushed forward his column from that point, for the purpose of either overtaking the invading rebel army, of intercepting it on its homeward retreat, or of arriving on the borders of Missouri in time to participate in the lively war scenes which were soon to visit that section.

The Ninety-fifth, during this expedition, was commanded by Lieut. Colonel William Avery, Colonel Blanden having been ordered North on recruiting service, while the regiment was at St. Charles. The line of march was northward from Brownsville, through north-eastern Arkansas, passing through Austin, Sircy and Pocahontas, and crossing the White, Little Red, and Black rivers, and the movement throughout was conducted by General Mower with all the energy and celerity for which that dashing officer was characterized. The regiment were required to sound the reveille at an early hour each morning, dispose seasonably of their hard-tack and coffee, and start on the march long before daylight. The army moved forward each day promptly at the time mentioned in the orders, and all soon understood that the hour set for marching by the general commanding was to be literally observed and carried out with precision, and that if they desired to follow him as leader, they must hold themselves ready to move when he moved, which was invariably at the moment he had previously appointed.

After a long and tedious journey, day and night, through this section of country, in quest of Price, the troops, worn out by constant marching, and many of them barefooted, arrived at Cape Girardeau, Missouri, on the Mississippi river, above Cairo, October 4th, 1864.

Price, in his advance to Missouri, had taken a different route, and this column of Union troops under Mower, met with no serious opposition from the enemy during its march through to the Cape. There was occasional skirmishing by our cavalry at the front.

It was on this march that the officers and men of the Ninety-fifth conferred upon their worthy and good-natured commander, Colonel Avery, the honorable and fatherly appellation of "Colonel Pap." On starting out from Brownsville the usual stringent orders were in force in reference to foraging and pillaging. Regimental commanders were held strictly responsible that these orders were executed. On this trip, many of the Ninety-fifth men broke over the rigid rules and regulations, and as the regiment filed into camp at night, they often appeared, in common with the men of other regiments, well loaded with articles which would go far toward satisfying hunger, and in connection with the monotonous hard bread and coffee, make a desirable, if not a sumptuous evening meal. The division commander having noticed these things, one day mentioned the matter to Colonel Avery, and requested that he prevent his men from foraging by the roadside, as it was against orders and could not be allowed. Colonel Avery, however, contended that his men had foraged nothing since leaving Brownsville, that the boys supplied themselves at that point with the very articles which now excited the suspicion and displeasure of the division commander, and had simply brought them along for their comfort during the expedition. Whenever the colonel was spoken to by his superior officer in reference to this matter, his unanswerable argument was that his men transported their forage from Brownsville, and had seized nothing *en route.* For this cunning manner in which the colonel shielded his men from accusations of foraging which, if traced up, would, in many instances have been found true, and for many other kind traits which he exhibited during the expedition, they resolved that henceforth he should receive the sobriquet, "Colonel Pap," and ever afterward he was known among them by that title.

The troops halted but a few days at Cape Girardeau, as Price had already entered the State and penetrated to a point far north of them, evidently intending to strike Jefferson City. Their services were, therefore, needed at once in that direction. On the 7th day of October, the Ninety-fifth embarked on the steamer "Omaha" for St. Louis, arrived there on the 10th, and was here transferred to the transport "Yellow Stone," for a trip up the Missouri river to Jefferson City. After much delay in ascending this muddy stream, on account of numerous sand-bars in the river, the regiment reached that point October 16th, and on the 20th moved forward by railroad to Sedalia. It was here assigned to garrison duty, Colonel Blanden being in command of the post, and remained at Sedalia until the campaign against Price ended in the complete defeat and rout of that invader's army. While here, it was actively employed in receiving and forwarding the large numbers of prisoners continually coming in, under guard, from the front, among whom were the notorious rebel leaders, Marmaduke, Cabal, and many other officers of inferior rank. The whole Union army, after these successful operations, commenced moving back to St. Louis by easy marches, and the Ninety-fifth returned with Major General A. J. Smith's command, to that place, by way of Jefferson City and Hermann, arriving there November 11th. On the following day, General Smith's troops were assigned quarters at Benton Barracks, five miles out from the city. These were not to be their winter quarters, however, for the grand military movements then progressing in Tennessee demanded the immediate presence of General Smith's command in that State.

CHAPTER VIII.

Operations of Hood in Tennessee — His Advance on Nashville — Battles at Columbia, Spring Hill, and Franklin — General Smith's Command ordered to Reënforce General Thomas at Nashville — Leaves St. Louis on Transports, and proceeds to Cairo — Voyage up the Ohio and Cumberland Rivers — Safe arrival at Nashville — Detachments of the Ninety-fifth rejoin the Regiment — Account of the Georgia Detachment during General Sherman's Campaign — Active preparations made around Nashville to receive Hood — His Army in sight — The Ninety-fifth holds an important Position in the Defenses of the City — Work on the Fortifications — Thomas moves his Army out to attack Hood — Great Battles of December 15th and 16th, 1864 — Hood's Army defeated and driven back in confusion — Part taken by the Ninety-fifth — The Pursuit to the Tennessee River — General Smith's Troops ascend the river and go into Winter Quarters, at Eastport, Miss. — Expedition to Corinth — The Hard-tack Famine at Eastport — Corn issued to the Troops — The Boys desire to draw Halters — Arrival of Rations — Preparations for another active Campaign — Transports arrive to convey the Troops to New Orleans.

THE rebel General Hood, at the head of a large army, liberated as he supposed from General Sherman's grasp, who, leaving him to be looked after by General

Thomas, had commenced his great march to the seacoast, was now concentrating near the southern boundary of the State of Tennessee, and initiating a campaign northward, with the view of capturing Nashville, and sweeping forward successfully to the banks of the Ohio river. Major General Thomas, commanding the army and department of the Cumberland, with headquarters at Nashville, was assigned by General Sherman to watch Hood's movements and defeat his designs. He had under him the 4th and 23rd Army Corps, together with a cavalry force, and about the middle of November, 1864, these Federal troops, then occupying position on the Tennessee river, near Huntsville, Alabama, watching the approach of the rebel army of invasion, commenced withdrawing gradually before Hood's advancing columns, now superior in point of numbers, in the direction of Pulaski, Columbia, Franklin and Nashville.

Hood, emboldened by this giving way, and apparent weakness of Thomas' retreating army, followed rapidly in pursuit, and promised his soldiers that he would soon lead them victoriously into the city of Nashville. At Columbia, on the Duck river, thirty miles below Nashville, the Federal army, under the immediate control of General Schofield, made a stand and gave the enemy battle to retard his movements.

Shortly afterward, at Spring Hill, another engagement took place, in which there was heavy loss on both sides. The Union forces resumed their line of retreat on Nashville, and Hood, flushed with what seemed to him important successes, hurried forward his army, and recklessly hurled it upon the Federals, now strongly fortified at Franklin. Both armies here fought with indescribable desperation, and each suffered terrible loss. It was one of the bloodiest and greatest battles of the war. The regiments of Hood's army were frightfully mown down, as they charged and recharged the works held by our troops, who would not surrender them.

The victory at Franklin was with the troops of General Schofield, but in accordance with orders from General Thomas, who planned all the movements, the former subsequently retreated to Nashville with both the 4th and 23rd corps.

It was the desire and plan of the veteran Thomas to draw the impulsive rebel leader as far north and as near to Nashville as possible, even to its very gates, before dealing him a decisive blow. Thus he had employed the forces under General Schofield in enticing Hood a long distance from his base of supplies, in retarding, worrying, and severely punishing his advancing rebel hosts, until heavy and important reënforcements could arrive at Nashville, whence he then intended to hurl forth his combined force upon the rebel army.

It was to participate in these stirring scenes, and to reënforce General Thomas' army at Nashville, that the regiments under General A. J. Smith were sent forward soon after rendezvousing at Benton Barracks. They were allowed to rest there but a few days, for the men to receive pay and obtain clothing, when the order was received to prepare immediately for an active campaign in the field, which indicated that our destination would be Nashville. Every preparation was accordingly made to leave for the scene of military operations now culminating near that place. On the 23rd day of November, 1864, Colonel Moore's division of General Smith's command, embarked on transports at St. Louis, the Ninety-fifth being assigned to the steamer "Isabella." The river to Cairo was filled with floating ice, making navigation somewhat difficult and dangerous. After coaling at Cairo, the fleet ascended the Ohio river, passing Paducah, Kentucky, and arrived at Smithland, near the mouth of the Cumberland, on Sunday, the 27th of November. To this point the boats conveying the troops of Colonel J. B. Moore's division had the advance, and a halt was here made until the remainder of the fleet, containing the divisions of General McArthur and General Garrard could close up, prior to ascending the Cumberland river. Necessary precautions were also here taken to ensure safety, and guard against surprise by the enemy while passing up this narrow stream. A regular signal code of steam whistles was issued to the commanding officer of each boat, by which the approach of the enemy, the presence of his batteries, or any other danger, might be made known, and which was to indicate the landing and disposition of the troops in case of attack. It was expected that the expedition would meet with trouble before reaching Nashville, as Hood was rapidly advancing on the place, and would endeavor to cut off the various lines of communication centering there.

On the 28th day of November, the whole fleet, containing the three divisions of troops, left Smithland and steamed up the Cumberland, escorted by a gunboat, General Smith's head-quarters boat leading the way. According to the orders, the transports were to keep within three or four hundred yards of each other and observe that distance except when notified differently by the established signals. Occasionally the screaming whistle of General Smith's flag-ship, responded to promptly by the various boats, would bring the whole fleet into "close order," which indicated there might be danger of some kind ahead. No trouble or misfortune, however, attended this expedition during the entire voyage. The transports ran day and night, passed Clarksville on the 29th, and arrived safely at Nashville early on the morning of November 30th. They arrived none too soon, for on the day following, the great battle was fought at Franklin, twelve miles distant, and soon afterward Hood advanced his lines to within a short distance of Nashville, and effected a blockade of the river above and below the city. Early on the morning of arrival, the Ninety-fifth debarked from the steamer "Isabella," marched through the city, and out two or three miles to the camp assigned. Here were found several of its detachments which had long been absent, and of which some account must be given before proceeding farther.

The regiment, before leaving Brownsville, Arkansas, on the long march to Missouri, sent its sick men and those who would be unable to endure an active campaign, together with all surplus baggage, camp and garrison equipage, back to Memphis, to which place it was expected the regiment would return. A convalescent camp was formed here, in charge of Lieutenant Gilkerson, of Company "E," and afterward the detachment was increased by the arrival of recruits from the North, who came down, supposing they would find the regiment at Memphis.

After the close of the campaign against Price, in Missouri, Lieutenant Gilkerson was ordered to proceed with his detachment of convalescents and recruits to Nashville, where he arrived a few days in advance of the regiment, bringing with him all its camp and garrison equipage.

Another, known as the Georgia detachment, was also at Nashville, waiting for the regiment to arrive. It had been separated from the command for a long time, and consisted of the convalescents who were left at Vicksburg at the time the Red River expedition set out, and were soon afterward ordered up the river to Cairo, and of recruits obtained by the recruiting party which, in charge of Captains Loop and Nish, was sent North from Vicksburg, in the winter of 1863. On their return with these recruits, in May, 1864, they received orders at Cairo, Ill., to accompany the 17th Army Corps, then assembled at that point, and on its way to reënforce the Federal army under General Sherman, operating in Georgia. They were assured that their regiment, as soon as it could return from the Red River expedition, would be ordered to Georgia also, but, as has been seen, its destination was in quite another direction.

This detachment, numbering between one and two hundred men, under command of Captain (since

Major) Loop, and Captain Nish, embarked at Cairo, with the 17th Army Corps, May 12th, 1864, and proceeded up the Ohio and Tennessee rivers to Clifton. Here the corps disembarked and took up its line of march across the country for General Sherman's army, passing through Huntsville and Decatur, Alabama. Ten miles below the latter place, Rhoddy's Confederate cavalry appeared, and after a sharp skirmish, in which the detachment took part, were put to flight. Afterward, on this march, lively skirmishes occurred with the enemy near Warrenton and at a pass through the Blue mountains, known as "Buzzard's Roost Gap," when he was again routed. On the 8th of June the detachment arrived at Ackworth, Georgia, where the great movements under Sherman were then progressing, and the 17th Corps immediately took position in the Federal line of operations. On the 14th of June, Captain Loop was detailed as engineer officer for the 3rd Division 17th Army Corps, and Captain Nish subsequently commanded the detachment. It was attached to "Worden's Battalion," and took active part in all the advances, flank movements, skirmishes and actions which characterized this celebrated campaign. It was warmly engaged in the battles of Kenesaw Mountain, Chattahoochee river, Atlanta, Jonesboro, and Lovejoy Station, and in common with the whole army labored arduously and incessantly until the campaign closed with the final evacuation and surrender of the "Gate City" of the South. Its casualties, during these movements, were, one man killed in action, eleven wounded, and two taken prisoners.

After resting a few days from the active duties of the summer's campaign, General Sherman's army started on its celebrated march through Georgia to the seacoast, and there was now no prospect that the Ninety-fifth would be sent to Georgia. The men of the detachment serving there having been long without pay and clothing, and suffered many inconveniences from their lengthy absence, were all anxious to return to the regiment. Major Loop, Captain Nish, Captain A. S. Stewart, and a few of the men, were relieved, and rejoined the regiment while at St. Louis. Afterward, the whole detachment, except those who were on detached service at various head-quarters in General Sherman's army, and who accompanied him to Savannah, was ordered to report to and rejoin its command at Nashville. It had been there a number of days on the arrival of the regiment, and had been serving at the front, aiding in retarding Hood's movements toward the city.

By Dec. 1st, 1864, Hood, following up the Federal

army on its retreat from Franklin, approached with his forces to within a short distance of Nashville, and extended his lines from the river above the city, around to a point below, where he planted a battery and effected a blockade of the Cumberland. From the reckless manner in which he had hurled forward his troops at Franklin, and in the battles below that place, it was expected he would at once lead a general attack, and attempt to storm the works around Nashville. Immediately on the arrival of General A. J. Smith's command, it was assigned an important position in the Union lines of defense, and held the right of General Thomas' army, resting on the river below the city. Digging and intrenching were now instituted along the whole Federal line, and each regiment was required to throw up works in its own front. The Ninety-fifth occupied a position on one of the Pike roads, leading south from the city, and in one night built fortifications which covered the regimental line of battle. Day and night the work was prosecuted vigorously, and promptly each morning at five o'clock the regiments were in line of battle, near their fortifications, where they remained until daylight, awaiting an assault by the enemy. In a few days General Thomas' army had constructed a continuous line of works around the city, and was fully prepared for any attack by the confronting rebel forces.

The Union line of defense was provided also with powerful batteries, located at proper intervals on those natural bluffs which surround Nashville, and which were now used advantageously for the defense of the city, and to conceal the numbers and real intentions of the Federal army. During these hasty but efficient preparations by General Thomas, he caused many of the citizens to be pressed into service, for the time being, and obliged them to go out to the lines and help build the fortifications. To see the clerks and city dandies, and other non-combatants, provided with haversacks well filled with hard bread, and marched out to the front where an opportunity was afforded of developing their soft muscles by work upon the forts and other defenses, was the cause of much merriment among the boys in blue, and they were thankful for such temporary assistance. There was some dissatisfaction on the part of those thus summarily hurried from their peaceful business pursuits, but it availed nothing against stern military necessity. If they were unwilling to shoulder a musket and march forth to the defense of the country, they were at least obliged, in this emergency, to shoulder a pick-axe or spade, and lend a helping hand in constructing works which might rescue Nashville from the grasp of Hood.

Between the 1st and 15th days of December, frequent skirmishes took place between different portions of the two armies, whose lines were in plain view of each other, without bringing on any general engagement. During this time there was every indication that Hood intended to make an attack, but having failed to do so, General Thomas, having everything prepared, determined to move out with his whole army from the works at Nashville, fight Hood, and drive him from his strong positions around the city. The Federal army consisted of the 4th and 23rd Army Corps, General A. J. Smith's command designated as " Detachment of the Army of the Tennessee," a large force of cavalry, and some colored troops. The Ninety-fifth was assigned to the 2nd brigade, 3rd division of General Smith's force, Colonel J. B. Moore commanding the division, Colonel Blanden the brigade, and Lieutenant Colonel Avery the regiment.

On the evening of December 14th, orders were received for the troops to have reveille at five, and to be ready to move at $5\frac{1}{2}$ o'clock A. M., on the following morning. All understood that this order meant business on the morrow, for our march could not extend far before coming upon the watchful foe. At an early hour, on the 15th, the camps were astir, preparatory to marching at the hour indicated. It was a reveille, however, without music, for no beating of drums or playing of fifes was allowed, lest the enemy might distrust the designs of the Union army. The morning was very foggy, and continued so long after General Thomas'. army was under motion, serving as a complete deception to the enemy, who was little suspecting an attack on that day.

Thomas moved his main army out on the Hardin Pike, with a large body of cavalry in advance and on the flanks, and immediately deployed it for action. The detachment of the Army of the Tennessee occupied the right, the 23rd Army Corps the centre, and the 4th Corps and colored troops the left of the Union lines of battle. It was a magnificent sight to witness this vast army of infantry, cavalry and artillery move forward steadily and gallantly to the work in hand, confident that no opposing force could withstand its onward sweep. Hood's main works were but a few miles distant, and soon after the troops were formed in line, the battle opened lively between the skirmishers of both armies. By 11 A. M., the contest raged furiously along the whole lines, and the rebel batteries commenced playing upon the advancing columns. The batteries on the enemy's left were charged and carried by storm during the afternoon, by a portion of the cavalry, and by General McArthur's division of infantry. On every part of the line General Thomas' army was successful throughout the day, driving the enemy steadily back, taking battery after battery, many prisoners, and killing and wounding a large number of his men.

In the charge made by Colonel Blanden's brigade, during the first day's battle, across an open field, the Ninety-fifth became exposed to a raking fire from one of the enemy's batteries, which it supposed had been taken by our troops on the left, and for a short time was in imminent danger of being severely cut up by the solid shot thrown from this unexpected source. This battery was soon in our possession, the regiment advanced rapidly over the field and escaped with the loss of only one man, Corporal John Kennedy, of Company "A," whose left limb was taken off near the knee by a solid shot. In this charge, Colonel Moore's division captured two or three hundred prisoners, who had taken position behind a stone fence, as sharpshooters. Darkness only put an end to the struggle on this day, but when the curtain of night fell upon the contending hosts, hushing them to silence, it was plain that General Thomas, thus far, had been everywhere successful, and remained master of the situation. Yet the events of this day's battle had not decided the fate of either army; there was yet disputed ground in front of the Federal lines, and during the night of the 15th every preparation was made, on both sides, to resume the contest early on the following day. Entrenching parties were busy all night long, with the axe, pick and spade, and at early dawn, on the 16th, the battle opened again in all its fury. Hood having been driven back on the day previous, had withdrawn a short distance to an advantageous position, and the key-point of his whole line, on the second day's battle, was located upon and near the Brentwood Hills. On the morning of the 16th, General A. J. Smith's command occupied position directly in front of these works of the enemy, and now held the centre of General Thomas' army, the 23rd Army Corps having been transferred to the right. Heavy canonading and musketry were kept up from morning until 3 o'clock P. M., without material advantage to either side. General Thomas had ordered a general charge at that hour upon the enemy's works, and at the appointed time it commenced vigorously along his whole line. General McArthur's division of General Smith's command covered itself with glory on this occasion, and well earned the honor of carrying the enemy's key-point by storm. Responding to the order for a charge with deafening yells, they swept up the steep heights under a murderous fire, regiment following and supporting regiment, and after a sharp and decisive assault, gained possession of the Brentwood Hills. As soon as these strong fortifications were thus gallantly carried, Hood's army, defeated now at all points, broke and fled in confusion toward Franklin. At the close of the second day's battle nearly all of his artillery had been captured, a large proportion of his men taken prisoners, and his killed and wounded left strewn over the various battle-fields. It was a great day for the army under the brave and strategic Thomas, but a terrible one for the ambitious and fiery Hood and his forces, which he had supposed were invincible. After his defeat and flight, our cavalry moved forward in immediate pursuit, the same evening. The infantry bivouacked for the night near Brentwood Hills, and on the morning of December 17th, advanced on the "Granny White Pike," toward Franklin. The demoralized rebel army was now in full and rapid retreat beyond that place, and our pursuing cavalry were continually sending back prisoners, and occasionally a heavy gun, which the enemy had endeavored to take off.

On Sunday, the 18th of December, the Ninety-fifth arrived at Franklin, and camped on the south side of the town, near the place where the great battle had been fought a few weeks previous. On the 19th, the regiment resumed the pursuit from Franklin, passing through Spring Hill, the scene of a great battle during Hood's advance, and marched the same day to within eight miles of Columbia, situated on the south side of Duck river. On the 22nd it moved forward to Duck river, and encamped on the north side of it. General Smith's troops were delayed here until the 24th, waiting for the 4th Army Corps, which, in the pursuit of Hood's retreating army, held the advance of the Federal forces, to cross upon the pontoon bridges. After the battles around Nashville, the different divisions and corps pushed forward vigorously, each desirous of being foremost in the pursuit. Such was the enthusiasm and zeal throughout the Union army over the recent victories, that its march from the Nashville battle-fields to Duck river was turned into an eager strife between the corps to precede each other. The 23rd Army Corps had fought along this same route on its retreat a short time previous, and now appeared to claim the road in preference to the detachment of the Army of the Tennessee, which had been ordered to follow immediately after the 4th Corps. On several occasions it endeavored to pass the troops of General Smith's command, thereby somewhat confusing the order of march. This was not permitted, however, on the part of General Smith and his men, who, at all times, maintained their position in the column, and gave their friends of the 23rd to understand that "Smith's Guerrillas" had performed trips of this nature before, were well posted as to their rights and duties, and were not to be jostled out of the designated order of moving. The 23rd were, therefore, obliged to march in rear of the detachment of the Army of the Tennessee, to Duck river, and all attempts to precede it were made in vain. There was considerable strife, also, at this stream, between these two commands as to which should first cross. The 4th Corps was already over, and General Smith was ordered to follow next. He commenced doing so, when a portion of the 23rd Corps desired to occupy the pontoon at the same time. The fiery old general seeing this, posted himself at one end of the bridge, and with drawn sword, swore that not a man of the other command should pass until his own force had crossed. On the 24th day of December, the Ninety-fifth passed over, marched through Columbia, and went into camp three miles beyond the town, where a halt was made until the wagon train, which was delayed at the bridge, could come up.

The weather was now becoming very cold, snow had fallen, the ground was frozen, and many of the men, having worn their shoes through, marching on the hard Pike road, were in suffering condition.

The regiment spent Christmas, December 25th, a

cold and disagreeable day, as cheerfully as possible in their camp near Columbia, waiting anxiously for the train to arrive with the blankets and rations. Though the rebel army had been through this section twice within a short time, and nearly drained the country of supplies, yet the Union soldiers, by the exercise of their characteristic inquisitiveness, succeeded in securing from the neighboring plantations plenty of fowls and roasters, which, in connection with hard-tack and coffee, furnished the officers and privates with respectable Christmas dinners. On the 26th, the regiment broke camp and resumed the march on the Pike, leading to Pulaski. All along the route were strewn the numerous evidences of the hasty and panic-stricken manner in which the demoralized rebel army retreated. Broken fire-arms, knapsacks and burdensome clothing had been abandoned by the foe in his precipitous flight, and were the sure indications of his terrible discomfiture. The infantry reached Pulaski, December 27th, where the solid Pike on which the troops had marched from near Nashville, terminated, and thence to the Tennessee river their course was to be over a dirt road, muddy, snowy, badly cut up, and difficult to travel at this inclement season of the year. In the pursuit thus far, the infantry had not been required to support the cavalry, which was far in advance pressing closely the fleeing and scattered rebels. Every day large numbers of prisoners were sent back from the front, and the cavalry needed no assistance in the prosecution of their good work.

The history of the war will not present an army worse beaten, cut up and disorganized than was Hood's at this time. The active campaign may be said to have now ended, though much severe marching was afterward performed before reaching the Tennessee river. The cavalry and the 4th Army Corps continued the pursuit in the direction of Florence, Alabama, where remnants of the rebel army succeeded in crossing the river and effecting an escape. The detachment of the Army of the Tennessee was ordered from Pulaski across the south-western portion of the State, to strike the Tennessee river at Clifton, and the 23rd Army Corps subsequently followed to that point. On the 28th day of December, the Ninety-fifth started from Pulaski and marched ten miles. Owing to the bad condition of the roads the troops were obliged to move slowly, and much difficulty was experienced in bringing up the wagon trains. The portion of country through which the army was now passing was the poorest section of Tennessee, had long been desolated by the ravages of war, and was now deserted mostly of inhabitants. Being in close proximity to the

Alabama border, it had felt the effects of the war much more severely than other localities of the State, and had been overrun frequently by both the Union and Rebel armies. Withal, it was the most loyal portion of Tennessee, and had sent forth* from its poor white communities important aid to assist in putting down the rebellion, a cavalry regiment having been raised in this section for that purpose. On the 30th of December, the Ninety-fifth moved on through Lawrenceburg, formerly of some importance as a manufacturing town, but now deserted and inactive. The following day was the severest which the regiment ever experienced in the service. During the night of the 30th a rain set in, which, by morning, turned into a cold snow storm. The troops suffered bitterly that night, and were ordered to proceed, at 7 o'clock the next morning, over the frozen roads. Many of the soldiers had worn their shoes completely through, before leaving the Pike at Pulaski, and a new supply could not be obtained until the army should arrive at Clifton. In this pitiable condition, many a soldier could be seen tramping along during that bitter cold day, while the very blood reddened his footprints on the snowy ground, as he passed along! I remember seeing, on that frosty day's march, a number of men belonging to the 44th Missouri Infantry, plodding along barefooted over the frozen roads, and there were similar instances in every regiment.

The 44th had been in the service but a short time, was hotly engaged at the battle of Franklin, where it was badly cut to pieces, and after the retreat to Nashville was immediately assigned to Colonel Blanden's brigade. It had started out on the present campaign without having time to obtain a sufficient supply of shoes and clothing. Its condition was, therefore, now deplorable, and it suffered extremely during this cold and tedious march in midwinter. The other regiments were better prepared at the outset, but all were obliged at this time to undergo much privation and suffering.

On the 2nd day of January, 1865, the Ninety-fifth started early from camp, near Waynesboro, and after a lengthy and fatiguing day's march, arrived late in the evening at Clifton, the present destination of General Smith's command. Thus finally ended the severest campaign in which the Ninety-fifth was ever engaged. When the suffering which prevailed in consequence of the extreme cold weather, and all the other circumstances are considered, it is believed there is no expedition in which the regiment participated during the service, which can compare with this one in point of suffering and fatigue.

After leaving Pulaski, nothing was seen of the retreating rebel army, on the route taken by General Smith's troops. What remained of it after crossing Duck river at Columbia, fled on another road in the direction of Florence, Alabama, closely pursued, as already stated, by our cavalry and the 4th Army Corps. The regiments rested at Clifton for a few days, and meanwhile transports arrived from Nashville, bringing plenty of shoes, clothes and rations for the troops. The weather continued cold while here, and the men had hard work to keep warm around their camp fires and beneath the thin-roofed "dog tents." In a few days General Smith's whole command were on their way up the Tennessee river to Eastport, where they were ordered to go into winter quarters. The second division (General Garrard's,) and a part of the first, commanded by General McArthur, had arrived at that point by the 8th of January, and on the same day Colonel Moore's division embarked on transports at Clifton for that place. The Ninety-fifth broke camp at Clifton late in the afternoon of January 8th, and proceeded to the river for the purpose of embarking. The different boats assigned to the two brigades of Colonel Moore's division were lying there, but were already heavily loaded with the transportation of the 2nd division, and a portion of the troops of the 1st. It seemed impossible to crowd another command of six regiments on the same transports. General Smith, in his characteristic manner, insisted that it could, and swore that it should be done. If any inferior officer attempted to argue with him the impossibility of carrying so large a force upon so few steamboats, at one trip, he would reply in his effective, though profane phraseology, that "These boats, sir, by G—d, sir, can carry these troops, sir, and five thousand more, by G—d, sir." Whether the brave old campaigner was worked up to this pitch of determination by a premeditated, sober intention and desire to debark his entire command that night, or whether he was laboring under certain other exciting influences on that occasion, it is unnecessary to consider here; but suffice it to say, that in accordance with his emphatic commands, the regiments went aboard the transports in a lively manner, crowding every nook and corner of the heavily freighted crafts. The place of embarkation was disadvantageous, being by a very steep bank, where the steamboats could be reached only along a narrow roadway leading down to the river's edge. A large quantity of the transportation belonging to another division, occupied this avenue of approach to the steamers, and had to be loaded before anything from Colonel Moore's command could gain admission.

Long after dark the Ninety-fifth, much delayed by

the confusion in which all things seemed to move, finally succeeded in getting aboard the steamer "Leni Leoti." To realize the scene on this occasion, one needs to have been present and witnessed it. Such an operation by daylight is generally attended with much wearisomeness and clamor, but when performed in a dark night, as at Clifton, presents one of the roughest scenes in army life, and is characterized by nothing particularly pleasant and attractive. It seemed to matter little, how much inconvenience one party caused another, in the general disposition of everybody to look out for number one. Different commanders wrangled and claimed the same boats exclusively for their own commands; those persons versed and expert in the profane tongue, found it an admirable occasion for exercising their versatility in that respect with great force and profusion. Soldiers were crammed into places where they perhaps had room to stand, but not to lie down; mules were knocked around and severely beaten, when, in fact, they knew more than those who were beating them; everything was in uproar, everybody was mad, and *somebody* must have been drunk. Spurred on by General "A. J.'s" stern orders, the troops completed their rough and tumble embarkation late in the evening of January 8th, and thus was verified his forcible assertion, that "it could and should be done to-night, sir."

The fleet moved up the river about midnight, passing Pittsburg Landing the 9th. Near this place guerrillas showed themselves, and delivered a few shots at the passing transports. The Ninety-fifth replied with volleys from the "Leni Leoti," and the infestors of the river bank suddenly disappeared under cover of the neighboring thicket. January 10th, the transports arrived safely at Eastport, and Colonel Moore's division commenced debarking early on the same day. The weather was stormy and cold, and the ground at the landing deep with mud. The regiments moved from the boats and remained near the river, on the wet and disagreeable low lands, until permanent camping-grounds could be selected, on the hills near by. In the afternoon camps were assigned, and the various regiments marched away to their respective encampments. The position occupied by General Smith's troops on the Eastport heights, was important and commanding, and a strong line of fortifications was thrown up immediately on the arrival of his divisions at that place, each division being required to fortify its own front.

Orders were now received for the regiments to build winter quarters, and all were soon busily employed in felling the thick timber and constructing the rude but substantial and warm log huts. In a few days the camp of the Ninety-fifth was changed into a miniature village, and the men were thus well protected from the cold, raw winds which, at that season of the year, continually sweep over those bleak hills.

On the 17th of January, the quiet and monotony of life in winter quarters was disturbed by an order for Colonel Moore's division to make a reconnoisance in the direction of Corinth, which was reported to be still occupied by a brigade of rebel cavalry, commanded by Ross. The object of the present expedition was to feel of the enemy, and, avoiding a general engagement, to ascertain whether or not he intended to hold his position at Corinth. Accompanied by a brigade of Federal cavalry, under General Croxton, the infantry moved from camp at Eastport, at 6 o'clock A. M., on the 18th, provided with three days' rations in haversacks and three in wagons, passed through the village of Iuka, and marched sixteen miles, camping fourteen from Corinth that night. Our cavalry during the day had some skirmishing with the enemy, who was easily driven back. The march was resumed early on the following day, and the head of the infantry column, then held by the Ninety-fifth, arrived in Corinth at noon, meeting with no resistance. The enemy, learning of our approach, had evacuated the place a few hours previous to our arrival, and had set fire to the "Tishiningo House," which was filled with rebel commissary stores. The building was still burning as we entered the town, and could not be saved. The troops halted in Corinth an hour or two for the men to make their coffee, and the object of the reconnoisance having been accomplished, the expedition turned back the same day in the direction of Eastport, marching out nine miles. January 20th it reached Iuka, and on the following day the regiment came back and resumed their winter quarters at Eastport. This expedition took place during delightful though chilly weather. The roads were hard and in good condition, except when they led through intervening swamps. The men of the different regiments who had been lying in camp for some days without much exercise, were greatly benefited by this march. The troops now experienced severe winter weather at Eastport, but the glowing camp-fires within the soldiers' snug log cabins, made everything comfortable and cheerful, and kept the men from freezing.

About this time, also, the rations for General Smith's entire command commenced growing short. Boats containing commissary stores were daily expected up the river, but failed to arrive, and soon it became necessary to provide measures against impending suffering and starvation. It was severe to oblige the troops to encamp upon those cold, bleak hills in midwinter, but when the prospect of being pinched for food was added to this, they considered the condition of affairs unnecessary and outrageous. Still the boys did not grumble much at their lot, but were rather disposed to make sport of their straightened and half-famished circumstances.

Several days passed, and the transports still failed to report with rations. There was something wrong somewhere down the river. Somebody was to blame, yet no one could tell where the responsibility for the delay rested. Finally the scant rations of the troops were all consumed, and immediately something had to be furnished the men for food. It happened that a large quantity of forage had been brought up the river for the horses and mules of the army. This was now used to prevent starvation among the troops, and as a dernier resort, shelled corn was issued to them by the bag full, in lieu of their regular rations. Some of the commissioned officers, whose messes had not been well supplied beforehand, were reduced to the same predicament with enlisted men, and were provided with the same article of subsistence as the soldiers. For a few days the troops had scarcely any other food to live upon, and corn-cake and popped corn were the only dishes afforded at the mess tables. Various jokes and hits were perpetrated by the boys upon those in authority, and they often wanted to know "when 'Old A. J.' was going to issue rations of *hay*, and draw *halters* for them." It is but just to state here, however, that neither General Smith, nor any one else at Eastport, was blamable for the scarcity of provisions, though there must have been a great fault somewhere in the commissary department of the army. There was no excuse for the uncomfortable condition of affairs, as ever since the arrival of troops at this point the line of communication had been constantly open to Nashville, the depot of supplies for the Army and Department of the Cumberland.

There is nothing about which a soldier is more sensitive than his appetite, and he very much dislikes to have it restrained or interfered with, unless under some great and pressing military necessity. He will go months without receiving a dime of pay, without a murmur, but place him upon short rations for a day even, and you will hear from him immediately. If you expect him to march, fight, or perform well in any manner, you must keep his haversack well supplied with at least hard cracker and coffee, or give a good explanation why it cannot be done. He never expects luxuries to be dealt out to him, but always insists that his regular rations, under ordinary circumstances, *shall be*, and if they are not forthcoming, he is liable to indulge in some of the most emphatic, caustic and often irreverent remarks concerning those in authority, which can be found in the soldier's vocabulary.

Finally, boats reached Eastport bringing large supplies of commissary stores, removing all fears on the subject of starvation, and thereafter the men had plenty to eat. It may be remarked here, that the story which appeared about this time in a Northern paper, representing that a transport having arrived at Eastport heavily laden with corn, the half-starved soldiers rushed violently on board and devoured the entire cargo, was wholly fictitious, having no foundation in fact.

While the Ninety-fifth was in camp at Eastport, Company "K," which, for a long time had been performing garrison duty at the mouth of White river, Arkansas, having been left there in the fall previous, rejoined its command. It had endeavored to report to the regiment at Nashville, but on its passage up the Cumberland river, had been obliged to disembark at Clarksville on account of the blockade, and was unable to meet the regiment in time to participate in the battles around Nashville, and the subsequent pursuit of Hood's army to the Tennessee river.

The troops remained in winter quarters at Eastport until the fore part of February, 1865, when a large fleet of transports came up the river for the purpose of conveying General Smith's command thence to New Orleans, where an expedition was then collecting and preparing, under General Canby, for a general movement against Mobile city.

CHAPTER IX.

The Ninety-fifth embarks on the "Adam Jacobs" for New Orleans — Fleet proceeds down the Tennessee River — Arrival at Cairo — Depredations committed there by the Troops — Voyage down the Mississippi — General Smith's forces disembark at Vicksburg — Afterward proceed to New Orleans — Disagreeable Camp below the City on the old Battle-fields — Regiment goes to Dauphine Island by way of Lake Pontchartrain — Arrival at the Island — Expedition of Colonel Moore's Brigade to Cedar Point, and up the west side of the Bay toward Mobile — Oysters and Musquitoes at Cedar Point — Advance up the Country — How the Music was used to deceive the Enemy — The 44th Missouri Band — Return of the Brigade to Cedar Point — Crosses the Bay, and rejoins 16th Army Corps at Dauley's Landing, on Fish River — General Canby's Army advances on Spanish Fort and Blakely — Investment of both Places — The part performed by the Ninety-fifth in the Reduction of Spanish Fort — Both Strongholds taken by Assault — Fall of Mobile.

On the 6th day of February, 1865, the Ninety-fifth embarked at Eastport on the steamer "Adam Jacobs," for the long journey to New Orleans. All the troops were aboard their respective transports by evening, and 6 o'clock the following morning was the hour set for departing. Promptly at the time ordered, the long whistle sounded from the general's flag boat, the boats swung out into the stream, and following each other in the order assigned, steamed down the Tennessee for their place of destination. The fleet arrived safely at Paducah, Ky., on the morning of the 8th, and proceeded down the Ohio to Cairo, where the transports remained until the 10th, taking on coal. The first division, under General McArthur, and the third, under Colonel Moore, arrived here nearly at the same time.

Regimental, brigade and division commanders now experienced much difficulty in keeping their commands on the boats, and were unable to prevent the commission of depredations on the private property of citizens, by a few mischievous and unruly soldiers. It is believed, however, that the Ninety-fifth had nothing to do with these troubles, and that its men conducted themselves while at Cairo as good soldiers. The same may be said of the 81st Illinois, and the 44th Missouri infantry, the other regiments of Colonel Blanden's brigade, whose men were likewise free from participation in the misconduct which may have occurred while the boats were stopping at that point.

At five o'clock A. M., February 10th, the fleet was again under way, and moved down the Mississippi, which was now full of large cakes of ice. After getting below Columbus the ice disappeared, the weather became mild, and the voyage was pleasant. The regiment arrived at Memphis, Feb. 11th, and on the following day resumed the journey. The fleet reached Vicksburg on the 13th, and landed below the city, by the flats. Instead of proceeding directly to New Orleans, orders came to disembark at this place, and General Smith, leaving his command at Vicksburg, proceeded to New Orleans, ascertained that an error had been made in transmitting the telegram, and that it was intended his troops should come directly to New Orleans.

Meanwhile, the regiments remained on the transports at Vicksburg until the 16th, when they moved off the boats, marched out in the rear of Vicksburg, and went into camp near the "four mile bridge," between the city and the Big Black river. Here they remained until the 19th, when orders came from General Smith to strike tents, move to the landing at Vicksburg, and reëmbark upon the same transports, which had been retained until General Smith could return from New Orleans. By the 20th everything was ready for a continuation of the voyage. The 2nd division, under command of General Garrard, which was left at Eastport, had now arrived, and at 4 o'clock

A. M., of that day, the whole fleet of twenty-four transports, conveying General Smith's entire command, proceeded down the river. The steamer "Adam Jacobs" arrived at New Orleans, with the Ninety-fifth, February 21st, and landed just below the city. The regiment remained on the steamer until the following day, when it disembarked and went into camp several miles below the city, on the old battle-fields of Jackson and Packenham. The grounds assigned here for camping purposes were of the worst character, being low, wet and muddy. The rainy season had commenced, and it was almost impossible for teams or men to move over the miry ground. It was the most disagreeable encampment the regiment ever had in the service, and all were glad when the order came to leave it.

While at New Orleans, General Smith's command underwent some changes in its name and organization. During its operations in the Department of the Cumberland, at Nashville, and throughout the subsequent campaign, it was designated as the Detachment of the Army of the Tennessee. On its arrival within the Department of the Gulf, it was formed into the 16th Army Corps, Maj. Gen. A. J. Smith commanding, and was known as such in the campaign against Mobile, and until the close of the war. The Ninety-fifth remained attached to the 2nd brigade of Colonel Moore's division, and other regiments were assigned to the corps at New Orleans, making it a very large and efficient command.

The regiments soon received orders to prepare for another active campaign, and early in the month of March, the troops began moving, some by the river and gulf, and others by way of Lake Pontchartrain, to Dauphine island, where the army, under General Canby, was assembling, preparatory to the general movement up the bay against Mobile. The Ninety-fifth was ordered to proceed to that point of rendezvous by the lake, and on the morning of March 11th, it cheerfully struck tents at the camp below New Orleans, and moved over to the old race course between the city and Lake Pontchartrain, where it was directed to obtain transportation and proceed directly to Dauphine island. The regiment bivouacked upon the track of the race course, which was perfectly dry and clean, and during the short delay here, the men enjoyed much more real comfort than they had experienced in the mud pastures below the city. Four companies of the Ninety-fifth, F, G, H, and K, were here detailed to remain and accompany the transportation of the division, and reported to Lieut. Nichols, A. A. Q. M., for that duty. On the 13th day of March, the remainder of the regiment, six companies, embarked at the Pontchartrain landing, on the steamer "Warrior," and in the evening of the same day started on the voyage. Passing through lake Borgne, and along the coast, the steamer arrived safely at Grant's Pass on the evening of the 14th, where she anchored for the night, it being a difficult place to navigate in the darkness. On the following morning she passed safely through, and landed at Fort Gaines, Dauphine island. The regiment disembarked and marched down the beach on the south side of the island, to the camp assigned. This was the healthiest locality which could have been selected for the encampment of troops. The men pitched their tents upon the clean sand, which was much preferable to New Orleans mud, were invigorated by the sea breezes, which came constantly from the gulf, and fared sumptuously on the oysters and fish, in which the island abounded.

At Dauphine island changes occurred in the brigade and division organizations. Brigadier General E. A. Carr assumed command of Colonel Moore's division, and the latter took command of the first brigade. The Ninety-fifth was transferred to it, and Colonel Blanden was relieved as commander of the second brigade by Colonel L. M. Ward, of the 14th Wisconsin infantry. Colonel Blanden had been commanding officer of the brigade ever since its formation at Nashville, had led it through the great campaign against Hood, and through all its subsequent wanderings, with much credit to himself as a military commander. Circumstances of rank, such as frequently occur in the army, now placed him once more in command of his regiment, which, for a long time, had been ably governed by Lieut. Colonel Avery.

The encampment of the troops on this healthy and favorable spot was to be short. There was work at hand, and active operations in that vicinity were soon to commence. Away up the bay, hid among her strongholds, and protected by fortifications, forts and torpedoes, which guarded all avenues of approach, lay the defiant rebel city, which, thus far in the war, had eluded the visitation and grasp of the Union armies. Silently she awaited the bursting of the storm gathering at her doors, and in the stupendous preparations culminating around her, was conscious of a fate similar to that which had befallen her rebellious sister cities, one by one, all along the Atlantic coast.

On the 18th day of March, Colonel Moore's brigade was ordered to cross over to Cedar Point, located opposite the island on the west side of the bay, and execute the first movement in the plan for capturing the city of Mobile. The Ninety-fifth and Seventy-second Illinois, 44th Missouri, and 33rd Wisconsin regiments, now composed the brigade, and embarking on steamers near the Fort Gaines Landing, proceeded to Cedar Point, accompanied by one section of artillery and two gunboats. Colonel Moore had instructions to effect a landing, advance in the direction of Mobile, and make such noise and demonstration as would convey the idea that the whole Union army was approaching by that route.

General Canby intended this as a feint merely, and during its execution he suddenly transferred the 13th and 16th Army Corps (except Colonel Moore's brigade) to a different point, and assembled them near Dauley's Landing, on the Fish river, on the east side of the bay. From this place the real and important advance was to be made against Forts Spanish and Blakely, the formidable outposts to Mobile, and the keys to the possession of the city itself. At the same time a strong column of white and colored troops, under General Steele, was moving from Pensacola, and sweeping around toward the same points.

The force sent over to Cedar Point landed without opposition, though on our approach mounted men were seen hastening away in the direction of Mobile. They belonged to a company of rebel cavalry, who were lurking in this vicinity, watching the movements of the Federal army.

Cedar Point was in plain sight of Dauphine island, had been formerly used as a place of encampment for rebel troops, and was still a point of military observation, where the enemy's scouts could watch from a look-out the Federal operations at the mouth of the bay, and whence they could quickly send intelligence to their authorities at Mobile. Important batteries had also been erected here in a former day by the rebels, intended to command Grant's Pass, but they had been evacuated since the great victory of Admiral Farragut, in Mobile bay, in the summer of 1864. There was no dirt soil in this locality, and these rebel forts were constructed entirely with oyster shells, which abounded here in superfluous quantities. The oyster-shell fortifications displayed something of a Yankee ingenuity, and to us who were accustomed to a different material, presented a novel and interesting appearance. The Ninety-fifth finished unloading from the steamer "Groesbeck," at Cedar Point, in the afternoon of March 18th, meeting with some difficulty in getting ashore on the pier, which extended into the bay, and which had been partially destroyed by the enemy in anticipation of the present movement.

The Seventy-second Illinois was the first regiment to go ashore, and just as the head of the regiment was stepping from the wharf, several large torpedoes were found concealed in good position for doing harm, but were discovered in time to prevent catastrophe to the command.

The Ninety-fifth camped that night on the point near the rebel look-out, and was ordered to be ready for a forward movement on the following day. The regiments were instructed to beat tattoo several times each, which would give the impression that a large Federal force had landed. The troops were now camped by the celebrated Cedar Point oyster-beds, and soon after landing here the surf was alive with wading soldiers, skirmishing not with rebels, but after oysters, of which they brought skiffs-full to the shore, and furnished the camps with large supplies of this luxurious article of food.

While the troops fared thus sumptuously on oysters during the brief halt made at Cedar Point, they also suffered greatly from the presence of annoying swarms of musquitoes. The soldiers had all seen musquitoes before, during the service, but never had they experienced such large-sized, ravenous insects of this nature, as these at Cedar Point. Oysters and musquitoes seemed to be the chief products of the locality, and the abundance and luxury of the one were equaled only by the multitudes and inflictions of the other. While the soldiers were satisfying their keen appetites as to oysters, the musquitoes were busy satisfying *theirs* as to soldiers; and while the boys in blue were feasting upon, and filling themselves with, the delectable food, these pestiferous insects were being filled with the blood of the intruding Yankees. These favorable and unfavorable circumstances commingled, did not continue long, however, and at an early hour on the following day, March 19th, the brigade moved forward toward Mobile. The Ninety-fifth held the advance of the column, and after proceeding a short distance, encountered the company of rebel cavalry, who had been watching the movements at Cedar Point. Company "A," of the Ninety-fifth, in charge of Lieut. Boyington, were immediately deployed as skirmishers, and the enemy retreated hastily.

The march was continued until dusk, when the regiments camped, in line of battle, in the thick pine woods several miles from Cedar Point. Orders were here issued for the regimental bands to beat three tattoos each, that evening, as well as a corresponding number of reveilles on the following morning, varying the tunes each time, in order to accomplish the deception intended. If this piece of strategy availed anything, it must have convinced the enemy that a large force of twelve regiments was approaching Mobile, whereas there were only four. An incident occurred here, however, which may have unwittingly carried information to the enemy of the real design of the expedition. The 44th Missouri had but recently formed a regimental drum corps, and the members composing it were unskilled in the art of blowing fifes and beating drums. On account of inexperience, their variety of tunes was necessarily small. Whenever they attempted the musical feat of executing the various changes of reveille or tattoo, the invariable result was a monotonous, discordant production, little worthy of the name of music. If you listened to them once, you could afterward easily detect them among a thousand well-trained bands. For this reason the drum corps of the 44th was not the best possible instrument with which to deceive the enemy in the manner proposed. At the hour designated for beating tattoo all the regiments played it through once, the musicians of the 44th performing it in their characteristic style. The second and third times, the tunes were varied by the other regiments, and one would have supposed that there were really so many more regiments in the Federal encampment. When, however, the 44th struck up its second tattoo, and attempted by continued musical demonstrations to represent another regiment, the failure was complete, and the boys throughout the different camps, unable to restrain themselves, burst forth in shouts of irrepressible laughter, making the woods ring for a long distance around. Thus this event, which furnished the men with so much merriment, may possibly have disclosed to the rebels the real character of the present expedition.

On the next day the brigade moved forward a few miles farther, to a small creek, where more torpedoes were found, and the artillery having made considerable noise in shelling the woods in front, the advance on Mobile by this route was discontinued, and the troops countermarched and returned to camp two miles from Cedar Point, where they remained during the 21st. In the afternoon of the 22nd, the Ninety-fifth embarked at Cedar Point, on the gunboat No. 48, crossed the foot of Mobile bay, and anchored that night near the mouth of Fish river. Early on the morning of the 23rd, the boats conveying Colonel Moore's brigade passed through Weeks' bay, a muddy and shallow body of water, and proceeded up Fish river eight miles, to near Dauley's Landing, where General Canby's army was now assembling. General Smith's corps had all arrived, and the 13th, under General Granger, appeared at that point nearly at the same time. The Ninety-fifth was in camp at Dauley's Landing only one day, and at an early hour on the 25th of March, both corps, led by General Canby in person, began the grand movement forward toward Forts Spanish and Blakely. The former was about eighteen miles distant, the latter twenty-three. The first day's march was ten miles, to Deer Park, where the troops halted for the night, and fortified, the advance divisions being required each night to throw up a line of works in their respective fronts. On the 26th the column again pressed onward, and leaving Spanish Fort a short distance to the left, camped that night within a few miles of Blakely. This was a feint, from which the enemy supposed that Blakely was to be immediately attacked, whereas Spanish Fort was to receive the first attention. Accordingly, on the morning of March 27th, the Union camps were aroused at an early hour, and the army, turning suddenly back, swept directly across to Spanish Fort. Brigadier General Carr's divison, of the 16th Army Corps, occupied the advance of the whole army, and were the first troops brought into action on this day. The rebel stronghold was only a short distance from the Federal encampment of the previous night. As the troops now approached it, heavy skirmishing commenced at the front, and the enemy appeared in force. Both corps were immediately deployed for a general engagement, and pushed forward in line of battle, through the thick woods, across ravines and over hills, the 16th Corps holding the right, and the 13th the left of the Union army.

Companies "A" and "D" were thrown out as skirmishers for the Ninety-fifth, and took active part in driving the rebels hastily back into their rifle-pits and fortifications.

The artillery opened fiercely on both sides, and soon the battle raged furiously all along the lines. By noon of the 27th, the Federal army had advanced to within close range of the enemy's main works, and the line of investment around Spanish Fort, from the bay above to the bay below it, was complete.

As Colonel Blanden's official report shows the important part taken by the Ninety-fifth, in the siege which followed, and which was prosecuted vigorously from March 27th, the day of investment, until April 8th, when the stronghold was taken by assault, and as the commissioned officers and enlisted men of the regiment have never had an opportunity of reading the regimental report of their doings and conduct during this sharp and decisive contest, I have thought it proper to incorporate the same herein for their perusal and benefit. It is as follows:

"Head-quarters 95th Regt. Ill. Inft'ry Vols., 1st Brigade, 3rd Division
16th Army Corps, near Blakely, Ala., April 10th, 1865.

"SIR,

"I have the honor to submit the following report of the operations of my command during the siege of Spanish Fort. On the morning of March 27th, when the brigade line of battle was first formed, I threw out my skirmishers, and the regiment immediately moved forward, skirmishing sharply with the enemy, and driving him back toward his works. By noon of the same day, my regiment advanced to within three hundred yards of his main line of works, and took position nearly in front of the "Red and White" forts, under a heavy fire of musketry and artillery, but without serious loss or injury among my men.

"My skirmishers were active during the remainder of the day, and at dusk, in compliance with orders from superior head-quarters, I set my men at work building the first line of works. The regiment occupied these on the 28th. . I then commenced digging a sap from this line across a ravine in my front, and by the 29th, my rifle-pits were completed to the opposite ridge, where the sharpshooters now advanced to within one hundred and fifty yards of the forts, compelled the enemy's gunners to close up the port holes with gabions and sand-bags, thus silencing effectually the heavy guns there mounted. After this, my command was busily employed, day and night, advancing our rifle-pits, under the constant fire of the rebel sharpshooters, and by April 8th, when occurred the final bombardment and assault by our forces, my trenches had been carried to within forty yards of the opposing line.

"During the furious bombardment opened by our artillery along the whole line, at five o'clock in the afternoon of the 8th, my regiment, with the exception of heavy details which were busy in front as sharpshooters and fatigue men, remained in camp, no order to the contrary having been received, until the rapid firing commenced on the extreme right of the whole Federal line held by Colonel Geddes' brigade of this division. In accordance with orders, I then formed my command in line, moved it at once into my advanced rifle-pits, raised the regimental colors over the works, and held my men in readiness for any movement. At this time the enemy, who had long been silent with his artillery, now expecting a general charge, opened with his heavy guns, and the cannonading became deafening and terrible. Having remained here between the artillery fires of both armies nearly an hour, I was ordered to move over to the support of Colonel Geddes' brigade, then charging the extreme left of the enemy's works, which it gallantly carried. I arrived at the point designated in time to coöperate, and remained in position there until late in the evening, when I received orders to move back to my own rifle-pits. I did so on the double-quick, and observing that Colonel Geddes' troops were advancing from the point already gained up the line of the enemy's works, and inside of them, I immediately led my regiment over the rifle-pits in my own front, and tearing away the *cheveaux de frise* in our course, charged the "Red and White" forts.

There were no other Federal forces preceding my command in the occupation of these works, and I pushed my line forward toward the bay, halting at the place where the brigade formed its line after the assault. I afterward advanced to within a short distance of the bay, company "B" being deployed as skirmishers, took possession of Fort Alexis, and placed proper guards over all heavy guns in that vicinity. In compliance with orders received long after midnight, I moved my regiment back to camp, where it arrived about 4 A. M., on the morning of the 9th, having captured two commissioned officers and thirty privates, prisoners of war, and a large amount of artillery. The men generally returned to camp that night, well loaded with flour, bacon, tobacco, etc., found in a rebel commissary building, which had been hastily evacuated.

"In concluding this report, I deem it but due to the commissioned officers and enlisted men of my command, to praise them for the brave, efficient and persevering manner in which they have conducted themselves from the beginning to the end of the investment. Where so many have performed their arduous duties so equally well, it is invidious to notice any distinctions of merit, and I have none to make.. Throughout the whole siege, they have labored almost unceasingly, by day and night, with pick and spade, as well as with arms, all intent upon accomplishing the common object.

"I herewith enclose a list of casualties occurring in my command during the siege just closed.

"I have the honor to be, Sir,

"Very respectfully, your obedient servant,

"L. BLANDEN,
"Col. Comd'g Reg't.

"CAPT. GEO. B. CARTER,
"A. A. A. Gen'l,
"1st Brig. 3rd Div. 16th Army Corps."

Thus, after a sharp contest of thirteen days, one of the most important defenses of Mobile, with four or five hundred prisoners and a large amount of artillery and small arms, fell into Union hands. Considering the space of time employed in reducing the stronghold, the investment of this place was fully equal to that of Vicksburg, though at no time was it so complete.

The rebel artillery was handled with great skill,

and was pronounced more effective than any ever before experienced in such operations.

In addition to their direct fire from formidable land batteries, during most of the time the water battery, known as Fort Eugee, located within close range, upon an island at the head of the bay, and their gunboats, were continually playing upon the Union lines, having from that direction an annoying enfilading fire, to which the right of the Federal army was particularly exposed. General Canby caused a battery of eight sixty-four pounders to be erected in a position commanding Fort Eugee, and in a short time her guns were silenced, and the gunboats driven farther up the bay, where they could do no harm.

While the investment of Spanish Fort was progressing, a portion of the besieging army, the 2nd division of the 16th, and the 1st division of the 13th Corps, were withdrawn and sent to reënforce the troops under General Steele, who had arrived from Pensacola, and had laid siege to Fort Blakely. After the fall of Spanish Fort, Blakely was the only remaining obstacle to the possession of Mobile city, and on the 9th of April a general assault was ordered upon that place. The troops which had taken Spanish Fort the night previous, were at once concentrated near there with instructions to act as a reserve to the charging columns.

At an early hour on the morning of the 9th, the Ninety-fifth was on its way for Blakely, arrived near there at noon and bivouacked in the reserve line of battle. Soon afterward the general assault commenced, and the fort was carried by storm without requiring assistance from the reserve troops. Between two and three thousand prisoners were here captured, and another large quantity of artillery and small arms.

These events, as predicted, determined the fate of Mobile. Forts Spanish and Blakely were her great points of guard, and when they succumbed she must likewise surrender. After they were taken, the Union iron clads could move up the bay to a close range, and reduce her to ashes in case she attempted to hold out longer. But she made no farther efforts at resistance, and on the following day after the capture of Blakely, the mayor of the city surrendered it to the military authorities of the United States. It was occupied by a portion of the 13th Army Corps, and soon the stars and stripes floated in triumph over the "Bay City of the South," and all her contiguous forts and strong places.

The campaign against Mobile was now at a close, and the presence of the 16th Army Corps, which had contributed so materially to crown the Federal arms with recent successes, was immediately required in another portion of Alabama.

CHAPTER X.

The 16th Army Corps ordered to Montgomery, Alabama — Rumors received before leaving Blakely, of General Grant's victories in the East — The suspicion with which the Ninety-fifth received flying reports, since they were deceived at "Big Sandy" — General Grant's success confirmed — Enthusiasm with which the Intelligence was received by the Regiments — The Ninety-fifth cheer lustily — The March through the Pine Forests — Guide-boards — A Rattlesnake Affair — Arrival at Greenville — The Ninety-fifth garrison the Town — Feelings of the Inhabitants — A Paper published by the Soldiers — March continued to Montgomery — Arrival there — General Wilson's Raid through this Section — Tooops camp around the City — Rebel paroled Soldiers from the Eastern Armies pass through — Beauregard, Bragg, Pillow, Semmes — Dick Taylor and Kirby Smith surrender — The Rebellion at an end — Drills resumed by the Ninety-fifth — What General A. J. Smith thought of their Dress Parade — Anecdote of the "Pointer Dog," and how Colonel Blanden came by it — Order from the War Department to Muster out Troops — The Men anxious to get Home — The 16th Corps retained for Garrison Duty in Northern Alabama.

DIRECTLY after the capture of Mobile, the 16th Army Corps received orders to proceed by land to

Montgomery, some two hundred miles distant, and on the 13th day of April it moved out from near Blakely for a long march to the first capitol of the Southern Confederacy. The route taken was over the old post line, traveled in times of peace, and lay through a dreary and almost interminable forest of pines, for which this section of country is celebrated.

Before leaving Blakely, vague rumors had reached us of the great battles between Grant and Lee, at and around Richmond, and a report circulated that the greatest rebel chieftain had surrendered with his entire army to the Lieutenant General of the Federal armies. Full confidence, however, was not placed in these flying rumors, and the 16th Corps was well on its way into the interior of the State, when news was brought by a courier from General Canby, at Mobile, confirming beyond doubt the glorious successes of the armies under General Grant, the capture of Richmond, and the entire overthrow of the rebellion in the East. The reliability of this intelligence was strengthened from the fact that General Smith, immediately on its reception, caused the information to be officially announced to each regiment of his command, and in response, the men made the silent old pine forests resound with their vociferous and oft-repeated cheers. It was on the 19th day of April that the great news was read to the Ninety-fifth, during a halt made for that purpose.

Now this regiment had, for a long time, and for good reason, been much opposed to cheering at reports of this nature, which were often originated and set afloat in camp, and on the march, by mischievous soldiers.

The members of the Ninety-fifth had, on a former occasion during the war, during the celebrated march from Grand Gulf to the rear of Vicksburg, cheered themselves hoarse over the premature news received and announced at Big Sandy, that Richmond had fallen; and ever since that well-remembered time, each man of the organization had vowed that he would never again be inveigled into an expression of applause for any man, or any thing, or any event, until he should first be satisfied as to the reliability of what he was applauding. Many times, therefore, when the other regiments would raise a shout on the march or in camp, at some supposed occurrence, the Ninety-fifth uniformly maintained silence, and the reminiscence of "Big Sandy" taught them better than to strain their lungs by useless and unrequited excitement.

But when this important intelligence, which had been whispered at Blakely, was now confirmed by an official dispatch from General Canby, who had received it direct from the War Department, the regiment, no longer doubting its truthfulness, broke over its long-established rule of taciturnity, and sent up such a succession of deafening cheers as the great occasion demanded.

The country through which this march was made, was the poorest portion of Alabama, only slightly cultivated in places few and far between, very sparsely inhabited by a few "poor whites," and was nothing but one vast, unbroken pinery and solitude, for the distance of more than a hundred miles after leaving Blakely. The distance to be marched was nearly two hundred miles, the weather was hot, the roads were hard and dusty, and many of the men were destined to be afflicted with sore feet before arriving at the journey's end.

It was reported at first that the troops would pass through Selma, and as the regiments were toiling along one day, some waggish soldier had posted a sign on a tree, where all passers-by could easily read it, bearing the following inscription: "To Selma, one hundred and fifty miles, *sore feet or no sore feet*," which the boys took as a good joke, but believed that the sentiment of their facetious friend contained much more solemn truth than poetry. Still farther on, another pioneer guide-board appeared in conspicuous position, having this announcement: "To *good living*, one hundred and ten miles," and the scarcity of chickens, pigs, and provisions of all kinds in this vicinity, and the abundance in which they were subsequently found, corroborated the entire truthfulness of the witticism.

Yet the men by no means suffered for want of plenty to eat, as a large wagon train followed the army, loaded with a sufficient supply of rations.

During the march through this pine region, one company of the Ninety-fifth decided that in the absence of the luxuries commonly found along the route of such expeditions, they would partake of a rare article of food which came into their possession in the following manner: the 44th Missouri Infantry, after getting into camp one evening, had slain a huge rattlesnake, which measured full six feet in length, and whose tail contained a dozen rattles. It was a monstrous reptile, fat, sleek and scaly, and its appearance demonstrated fully that if human beings could not find enough in that barren country to grow fat on, rattlesnakes *could*. The company of the Ninety-fifth, above referred to, procured the snake from the 44th Missouri, for the purpose of trying his fat and making a meal out of his flesh. Before sleeping that night it was served up for their supper, and was declared the most delicious repast they had partaken of for a long time!

After the march had been continued for a number of days through the almost unbroken wilderness, the army entered a more open and cultivated country, which presented many more evidences of cultivation and civilization than that through which it had been passing. The inhabitants along the line of march appeared more intelligent than the few denizens of the pine forests, whom we had occasionally met with since leaving Blakely. Having heard of the approaching Federal column, they now, on our arrival, professed loyalty, and in few instances displayed the American flag from their residences. At almost every house a white flag appeared, which denoted submission and friendship on the part of the occupants, and claimed protection for their premises. At the residence of one old lady, who appeared very patriotic, was to be seen hung up over her doorway the following device, printed in large, though rough, unsymmetrical letters: "The United States of America forever," and as the Ninety-fifth passed by, the band, at her request, struck up "Yankee Doodle," which seemed to please the aged matron exceedingly, for she had not heard that stirring national air in many a year, and, perchance, never before in her life.

On the 21st day of April, the advance of General Smith's command arrived at Greenville, formerly a thriving and beautiful village, forty-three miles from Montgomery. The Ninety-fifth was the first regiment to enter the town, and was assigned to perform all the provost duty therein, while the army halted and rested for a day near that place.

Much anxiety and fear was manifested on the part of the citizens, as the regiment took possession of the village, and quartered itself in the most important parts of it. The women cried, and supposed we had come to burn and sack the place. They soon had occasion to change their opinions, as guards were at once posted at each dwelling-house, order prevailed everywhere, and the timid inhabitants of Greenville, in a short time, acknowledged that they had never before during the war been so well protected, had never experienced such peace and safety as now reigned in their midst. They began to look upon the Yankee soldier with a more favorable opinion than they had before entertained of him from hearsay, and agreed that he was not such a fearful and destructive *beast* as had often been falsely represented.

The people were slow to believe the great news we brought concerning the capture of Richmond and the surrender of Lee's and Johnston's armies. They deemed it incredible and impossible, but after the soldiers, by General Smith's order, took possession of the

Greenville Observer printing office, and published the whole official correspondence which had occurred between Generals Grant and Lee, then their confidence and belief in the safety and success of their cause subsided, and they unwillingly accepted the truth that the great armies of the rebellion were fast disbanding, and that the last days of their attempted Southern Confederacy had indeed come.

While the army was resting at Greenville, General Grierson's cavalry arrived, and brought news fully confirming and placing beyond possibility of doubt the success of the national arms at all points, which insured the speedy return of peace to the land. On the 23rd day of April the troops moved forward now through a more open and much finer country than heretofore, and arrived at Montgomery on the 25th of the same month, having performed the whole journey from Blakely in thirteen days. The Ninety-fifth was the second regiment in the advance, and as the army marched through the city, with banners unfurled and music playing the national airs, the citizens gathered along the streets, to gaze at the first Federal infantry troops that had ever penetrated so far in that direction. General Wilson had made his celebrated cavalry raid through this section of the country a few weeks previous, had swept through the important rebel posts of Selma and Montgomery, and onward to Columbus and Macon, Georgia, destroying all works, buildings and supplies used in the interests of the rebellion, cutting important railroad communications and making his whole triumphant march a line of continuous devastation. In the important cities of Selma, Montgomery, Columbus and Macon, and at many intervening points, he and his men left numerous evidences of the hurtful manner in which they had dealt with rebellion in that portion of the Confederacy. They performed their work thoroughly and speedily, and truthful history will treat this grand cavalry movement as one of the boldest, most successful and most important undertakings of the war.

General Smith's forces, therefore, on arriving at Montgomery, met with no opposition. Everything had been well attended to by Wilson beforehand. He had stricken the people with terror, and cowed them into submission; they had already experienced sufficient effects of war in endeavoring to resist his advance, and no effort was now made to prevent the 16th Army Corps from occupying the city, and, with it, all of Northern Alabama. The various regiments went into camps assigned near the city, all tired and sore-footed, and thankful to have reached once more a permanent resting-place. Soon after arriving here, large numbers of paroled prisoners of war from Lee's and Johnston's armies began passing through Montgomery, seeking their respective homes. Day after day a continuous stream of Southern officers and enlisted men, who, during the past four years had been fighting for, and endeavoring to maintain, a causeless rebellion, were now coming back, defeated, crest-fallen, satisfied with war, glad that it was ended, and apparently no longer of rebellious spirit. Among them were such noted individuals as Beauregard, Bragg, Pillow, Admiral Semmes, and others, not now leading back large and well-organized armies, nor accompanying them from victorious battle-fields to the enjoyment of an accomplished rebellion, but returning disappointed and unattended to their homes, where, during the remainder of their lives, they are to experience that ignominy and shame which will ever attach to them as original and persistent traitors to their country.

Soon after the capitulation of Lee and Johnston in the East, came the intelligence that Dick Taylor had surrendered his Department to General Canby, which closed out the Confederacy from the Atlantic ocean to the Mississippi river. Then, finally, Kirby Smith, commanding trans-Mississippi rebeldom, following the example set by the Eastern rebel leaders, and deeming it useless to longer protract the struggle, delivered up his important command to the Federal authorities, and armed rebellion no longer existed within the boundaries of the United States.

The great work of crushing the rebellion was now complete; the tedious campaigns of the Union armies were accomplished, and the oft-repeated command, "Prepare for an active campaign in the field," was to be announced no more to the troops. The only duties remaining to be performed by the 16th Corps, were the collection of the Confederate property, of which a large quantity was scattered through Northern Alabama, and the maintenance of good order in society, which, from the absence of either civil or military authority in many portions of the State, was in deplorable condition.

The encampment of the Ninety-fifth while at Montgomery was located about three miles north of the city, on the road leading to Macon, Georgia. Here a beautiful camp was chosen in the woods, and as there was a prospect of remaining at this place for some time, much pains were taken to make it clean and comfortable. A chapel was built under the trees near the center of the encampment, where Divine services were held regularly every Sabbath, and frequently during the week, by James H. More, as chaplain of the regiment, who always took great interest in the spiritual welfare of the men, and by his Christian zeal and perseverance, exerted a beneficial influence over all with whom he was associated. After becoming well rested from the lengthy march recently performed, the regiment resumed battalion drills and dress-parades. The men could not see the need of farther drilling, since the war was over and there was to be no more campaigning; yet their duties in camp were light, and a continuance of good health in the command demanded the revival of such exercises. After a few days, however, battalion drills were discontinued, while dress-parade was kept up and held regularly each evening.

From constant practice since arriving at Montgomery, the regiment had attained a great degree of proficiency in this exercise, and the men executed the various commands in the manual of arms, with such precision and concert of action, that it elicited the praise of distinguished military officers of the regular army.

On one occasion Major General A. J. Smith, the Corps Commander, was present, and witnessed the Ninety-fifth on dress-parade. The men did their best in the presence of the veteran whose eye was upon them, and after the parade was over, he remarked that he had never seen the Cadets at West Point excel this military performance of the Ninety-fifth.

While the regiment was lying in camp here, many of the officers and men of the Ninety-fifth and other regiments, in view of the probability that they would soon be allowed to muster out of the service and return to their homes, were desirous of taking back with them from the South some relic — some curiosity, animate or inanimate, peculiar to the Southern soil and climate. In making such selections there was a great diversity of tastes. Some chose shot-guns; some, rebel swords; some, caged-up birds, of various kinds; while not a few of the officers and soldiers (among whom may be mentioned the names of Colonel Blanden, of the Ninety-fifth, and Captain Frank G. Hopkins, of the 44th Missouri Infantry,) were anxious to secure fine-blooded dogs, in which this section of the South abounded.

During the halt which the 16th Corps made at Greenville, on its way to Montgomery, Captain Hopkins, then in command of the 44th Missouri regiment, had procured a fine pointer dog, and brought him to Montgomery, with the intention of taking him North. Whether the animal was purchased, or strayed from the rightful owner and followed after the Captain at his solicitation, it is unnecessary here to decide; but, at least, the Captain considered that, having full possession of the property, his title was valid, certainly as against all other officers and soldiers. On arriving at Montgomery, he therefore kept him well secured at his head-quarters. One day, however, the dog released himself from this confinement, and by chance wandered over to Colonel Blanden's head-quarters, which were near by. The Colonel, unaware that it belonged to his friend, Captain Hopkins, and supposing it had strayed into camp from some neighboring plantation, decided to tie it securely near his own head-quarters, and congratulated himself on having found a valuable pointer dog, which he designed to take home with him. Several days passed, and the dog was still secure at the Colonel's head-quarters, unclaimed, and he now considered himself undisturbed in the possession and ownership of the property. One evening, after the Colonel had retired for the night and was fast asleep, a communication was received at regimental head-quarters, from Captain Hopkins, which read as follows:

"Head Quarters 44th Missouri Infantry Volunteers,
Camp near Montgomery, Ala., May 2, 1865.

"COLONEL: I have the honor to request that you permit the bearer to take charge of a certain '*pointer purp*,' said to be in your possession, which I claim to be owner of.

"The said animal is of the male persuasion, has a *double nose*, is liver-colored and white.

"Said 'dorg' strayed from my camp on or about Saturday, April 29th, 1865.

"Hoping you will comply with this modest request, I have the honor to be, Colonel,

"Very resp'y, your obed't serv't,
"Capt. FRANK G. HOPKINS,
"Commanding 44th Mo. Inf'y.

"Col. L. BLANDEN,
"Com'd'g 95th Ill. Inf'y."

The colonel was immediately aroused from his slumbers by the adjutant, who presented the communication, and desired to know what disposition should be made of it. The latter was instructed to send "the bearer" back to camp without the dog, and to return the captain's communication, with such strong endorsement as the circumstances of the case called for. At a late hour the same night, therefore, the following endorsement was written on the back of the captain's paper, and sent over to him about midnight:

"Head-quarters 95th Ill. Infantry Vols.,
"Camp near Montgomery, Ala., May 2nd, 1865.

"Respectfully returned to the commanding officer of the 44th Mo. Inft'y Vols., with the information that a 'Purp,' answering somewhat to the description contained in the within canine communication came to these head-quarters on or about April 29th, 1865, hungry, exhausted, and apparently without owner. The animal exhibited every evidence that it had not been long absent from some planter's home, and was not used to the ways and customs of the army. The thought then suggested itself that said pointer dog might, shortly since, have been the pet of some fair one at Greenville, and have strayed away through the enticing efforts of some mischievous soldier belonging to 'Smith's Guerrillas,' though the undersigned does not suppose for a moment that the within claimant formed his proprietary interest (if he has any) in said animal, in any such manner.

"The within-mentioned dog, since his advent to these head-quarters, has been well fed, well treated, and *well tied* to a tree near my tent, showing conclusively that his presence hereabouts has been open and undisguised, and consequently my possession up to the present date, has been of the most innocent character. In conclusion, I would say that the within description does not identify the animal in question with sufficient particularity, and it being too late this evening to determine all the points referred to within, I would therefore request a personal interview with the claimant, at these head-quarters, to-morrow morning, when he can prove property, pay charges, and take his ' Purp.'

"By order of

"L. BLANDEN,

"W. W. WOOD,   "Col. Com'dg Regt.

"Adj't."

The captain did not appear, however, on the following morning to press his claim. He was so much pleased with the endorsement in reply to his own communication that he had nothing more to say on the subject of dogs, and insisted that the colonel should remain in undisturbed possession of the "double-nosed pointer."

The regiments, after remaining at Montgomery a few weeks, all became anxious to be mustered out of the service, as they seemed to be no longer required, and they now desired to return to their homes as soon as possible. A general order from the War Department had been issued, authorizing all troops whose term of service expired before October 1st, 1865, to be mustered out and sent home immediately. In accordance with this order, the Union armies at the East were being rapidly disbanded or materially decreased.

The 16th Army Corps, however, was excepted from the operation of the order until late in the summer, and was scattered in different directions through Northern Alabama, doing guard and garrison duty, protecting society from marauders, and gathering in the Confederate property which had accumulated at different points, and which was now claimed and taken possession of by the Federal Government.

CHAPTER XI.

A portion of the 16th Army Corps sent to North-eastern Alabama — Col. Moore's Brigade garrison Tuskegee, Opelika, and Union Springs — The Ninety-fifth occupy Opelika — Feelings of the Citizens — Stringent Whisky Orders enforced by Col. Blanden — Management of the Negro Question — Paroled Rebel Soldiers — The Fourth of July, and how the Soldiers Celebrated it at Opelika — Officers and Men anxious to be Mustered Out — The Regiment relieved, and returns to Montgomery to be sent home — Proceeds to Vicksburg via Selma, Meridian, and Jackson — Arrival at Vicksburg — Takes Steamer up the River to St. Louis — Goes thence to Springfield, Ill., for final Payment and Discharge — Mustered out of the Service at "Camp Butler" — Return home to McHenry and Boone Counties — The Receptions there given the various Companies — Conclusion.

THE Ninety-fifth remained in camp at Montgomery, Alabama, until the 23rd of May, when Colonel Moore's brigade was ordered into the north-eastern part of the State for garrison duty, to preserve order in society, and to collect the property of the Confederacy remaining in that section. The 33rd Wisconsin and 44th Missouri regiments were stationed at Tuskegee, the county seat of Macon county, where Colonel Moore established his head-quarters; the 72nd Illinois at Union Springs, and the Ninety-fifth was assigned to occupy Opelika, a town on the railroad, sixty miles from Montgomery. The regiment arrived at Opelika on the 26th day of May, having had a hot and dusty march from Montgomery. The inhabitants of the place did not express many manifestations of joy at the location of Union troops in their midst, for now that the war was over, and the rebel armies disbanded, they could see no necessity for the continued military occupation of the country.

As the regiment marched through the village to its place of encampment, the houses were all kept closed; the fair occupants, incensed at our arrival, did not show themselves, and excepting a few Confederate paroled soldiers and citizens sitting around various rum-shops and places where business was formerly transacted, the town appeared deserted and lifeless. Opelika was a point where many of the paroled rebel soldiers, on their return homeward, had been in the habit of stopping, and using freely during their stay the commissary stores and other property which had been here collected by agents of the pretended Government for which they had so long and so unsuccessfully been fighting. These released prisoners considered that, in the general bankruptcy which had befallen their cause, they were entitled to a share of the plunder, especially as against their own citizens, many of whom were appropriating it to their individual use. The whisky trade was also carried on here quite lively, and was another cause for detaining crowds of soldiers as they came through from the East. There were several stills in this vicinity, where the beverage was produced in large quantities, being manufactured from corn, and, in character and effect, strikingly resembled the article which is known to endanger the life of an individual at the distance of forty rods. Colonel Blanden, on assuming command of the Post, deeming that the whisky traffic, if continued, would give him much trouble in the government of his own command, and in controlling the numerous Confederate soldiers who were continually passing along that route, issued an order closing up all saloons and prohibiting the sale of intoxicating liquor to his men by any one. The order was efficacious in closing the doors of the whisky-dealers. Good order soon prevailed, and little drunkenness was noticed thereafter in the streets. The Colonel was unable, however, to keep liquor from those of his own men who were in the habit of using it, and the stringent restrictions which he enforced, did not produce all the good effects intended, in the regiment. There were such a number of whisky-stills in the neighborhood, that liquor could be easily obtained from them, and was frequently brought into camp unbeknown to the commanding officer. It has been often remarked, by officers and men, that during the whole service never was so much inebriety known in the Ninety-fifth as while under the prohibitory regulations introduced at Opelika. If the Colonel could have struck at the source of the evil, and burned down or closed up effectually those places where the whisky was manufactured, then his policy would have proven more successful, and his drinking men been more temperate. But he came here with strict orders to respect all private property, and was therefore unauthorized to interfere with the rights of those who owned, and were running, the stills. His strong temperance principles would have impelled him, had he possessed the authority, to demolish those institutions, and abate them as public nuisances.

Soon after the arrival of the troops at Opelika, the negro question became the principal subject of consideration, and gave the military commander much trouble and annoyance. Up to this time the negroes in this section had continued to be held and considered as slaves by their former masters, who were loth to admit that the war had done away with their former relations and their cherished institution. The policy, however, of treating them as freedmen, which had been carried out in the Southern States by the Federal armies since President Lincoln's proclamation in 1863, was at once announced here to the people, and notice given them that, if they wished to retain their colored laborers, they must agree with them for their services and grant them just compensation for their labor. Large numbers of the colored people flocked in daily, anxious to learn what rights they had under the altered condition of affairs, and complaining, in many instances, of maltreatment on the part of their former masters. They were told that they were perfectly free, but were advised universally to seek employment immediately, either on the plantations where they had been living, or elsewhere.

The planters also appeared frequently at head-quarters with their complaints, representing their many inconveniences and sufferings consequent upon the release from bondage of the negro population. They were informed plainly, that the relation of master and slave no longer existed in Alabama, and that while the negroes would not be allowed to roam about the country unemployed, they would still be protected in all their privileges as freedmen.

The planters finally accepted the new policy with

reluctance, and for the first time in their lives were obliged to accommodate themselves to a new order of things, and practice the free-labor system.

Before the arrival of the regiment at this place, society in this vicinity was in very bad condition, there being neither civil nor military law in operation. Colonel Blanden applied himself diligently to the work of ferreting out certain criminals who had been disturbing the peace of society in the neighborhood, and forwarded several of them to Montgomery for trial and punishment.

During the time the regiment encamped here, Opelika was designated as a Post for paroling rebel soldiers. At the close of the war many of these were absent from their commands on furloughs and sick, and came in now willingly to obtain their paroles. Between two and three hundred were paroled, only *one* of which number expressed himself in favor of a continuance of the rebellion. The great majority of them seemed perfectly satisfied with the result of the war, and claimed that they had never been in favor of it, from the beginning. Many of these soldiers were honest in such assertions, and had been forced into the ranks by that reign of terror which the leading traitors instituted and carried out to advance their base schemes and sustain their rotten Confederacy.

William L. Yancey had been one of those prominent characters, who had precipitated his own State, and hastened others, headlong into the rebellion, and had incited the youth of the South to take up arms, for the accomplishment of his traitorous purposes. Though his body now lay entombed in the cemetery at Montgomery, no Alabamian was heard to speak well of his character as a politician or a man. He was never referred to by the citizens or paroled soldiers except in terms of reproach and hatred, and they looked upon him as the instigator of all their troubles, the prime mover in hurrying Alabama out of the Union. They claimed that the doctrine of secession, at the outset, would have been condemned by an overwhelming majority, had Yancey and his fanatical clique submitted the question to a fair vote of the people.

This was not done, and after the ordinance of secession had once been passed, the citizens excused their subsequent action in the war, on the false ground that their allegiance could no longer be claimed by the United States; that thenceforward it was due alone to the State; that the State was their country, and that their only alternative was to aid her in asserting the great Southern heresy of State Rights.

The results of the war had now taught these people a different doctrine, and from the sad and ruinous experience of four years' rebellion, they had learned the true strength and indivisibility of the American government. It is a lesson which will long remain fresh in their memories, and will descend to their posterity as a fearful warning against future attempts to dissolve and destroy the perpetual Union of States established by the fathers.

The summer of 1865 was passed pleasantly by the regiment, in the performance of their easy duties at Opelika. The locality was very healthy for the men; good water was abundant, and fruit, vegetables and all necessary eatables were easily obtained. Never before during the service had the command been so well provided for, and so free from sickness. The inhabitants, after recovering from the sulky disposition manifested on our arrival, and from the dissatisfaction which followed the enforcement of the policy in reference to the negroes, became resigned to existing affairs, appeared more affable, and made frequent visits to the encampment, to see and converse with the soldiers.

The Fourth of July was observed by the soldiers of the Ninety-fifth, at Opelika, in the old-fashioned manner. They had no artillery with which to arouse the inhabitants at an early hour; but long before sunrise of that day, the various companies formed at the camp, without reference to officers, and commenced firing a National salute with their muskets. It sounded like very heavy skirmishing in the rear of the town, and in war times would have indicated an immediate attack. Some of the citizens, awakened from their slumbers, knew not what to make of this unusual procedure, and feared that their lives and property were in jeopardy for some offense they had recently committed. Their apprehensions were allayed, however, on learning that it was only the opening exercise of the celebration of the Nation's birthday — a day which had long been disregarded and lost sight of by the people of this section.

The firing of the National salute continued vigorously until breakfast time, after which a large delegation from the regiment, in command of Quartermaster Sergeant Early, formed in procession at the encampment, and paraded through the principal streets of the village, bearing the American flag, and keeping step to patriotic music furnished by the regimental band. Brief speeches were made to the men by Col. Blanden, Major Loop, Quartermaster Southworth and Adjutant Wood, and the day was passed joyously and with enthusiasm, by all concerned. In the afternoon, a novel dress-parade was held at the usual place, in which none of the commissioned officers were allowed to take part. Sergeant Early, who had been chosen as leader of the boys that day, commanded the parade, while the positions of the different commissioned officers were filled from the non-commissioned grade, and other enlisted men. The whole affair was laughable to behold, yet all the movements were executed with great precision, and reflected much credit upon the temporary commander and his men.

The guns on this occasion were loaded with blank cartridges, unbeknown to the large number of spectators, white and black, who had assembled in front of the battalion to witness the exercise. At the command, "*ready — aim — fire!*" the pieces were all leveled and discharged in unison, making a terrible report, and scattering the crowd in front in various directions. The promiscuous assemblage of white people and negroes were badly frightened, but suffered no injury from the harmless firing of the blank cartridges. At the conclusion of the parade, Col. Blanden presented the sergeant in command with twenty dollars, which was well used in closing up the festivities of the day, and all felt satisfied with the manner in which it had been celebrated.

The officers and men of the regiment were now becoming uneasy on account of being detained in the service, as they deemed, unnecessarily. There was undoubtedly need of some military force in that section to preserve order in society, but it was thought that one company would have performed all the necessary duties at this post, and answered fully as well as a whole regiment. Beside, it was claimed that there were plenty of veteran troops in the corps, who could be sent to relieve those whose term of service would expire before October 1st, 1865. The commanding officer of the department, however, knew best what forces he needed to retain in his command for the military government of the State, and doubtless forwarded the regiments to the rendezvous appointed for mustering troops out of the service, as soon as their services could be spared.

On the 15th day of July, orders finally came for the regiment, on being relieved by three companies from the 52nd Regiment Indiana Infantry Volunteers, to return "by land" to Montgomery. The new force arrived on the 17th, took charge of the place, and on the following day the Ninety-fifth bade adieu to Opelika, and started on their homeward journey. It had been hoped that the regiment would be sent by railroad from Opelika directly to Louisville, Ky., a much cheaper route for the Government and far easier for the soldiers, as by this route there would be no marching. It was ordered otherwise, and the course of the regiment from Montgomery was destined to be across the country to Vicksburg, the place designated for muster-out.

Instead of returning to Montgomery entirely "by land," as directed in the order from superior headquarters, the soldiers determined they would make some of that distance "by rail," at the risk of being reprimanded for disobedience of orders. A train was chartered, which carried the command twenty-five miles to Chehaw Station, thus saving the men a tedious and sultry march. The weather was so excessively hot that the troops could only move a short distance during the day, and most of the marching had to be done very early in the morning. From Chehaw Station, the regiment, under command of Major Loop, marched to Tuskegee, where it was joined by the 44th Missouri and 33rd Wisconsin, belonging to the same brigade. From this place the three regiments moved forward, July 19th, and on the following day were joined by the 72nd Illinois Infantry near Line Creek, which regiment had just been relieved from duty at Union Springs. The brigade arrived at Montgomery July 21st, and the regiments resumed the respective camping grounds which they had left in the latter part of May previous.

The troops were now sent forward for muster-out at

Vicksburg as fast as transportation could be furnished down the Alabama river.

The Ninety-fifth was delayed several days at Montgomery, and meanwhile the company commanders employed the time profitably in preparing their muster-out rolls. A large number of recruits whose terms of service did not expire with the organization, were here formed into a detachment and left in charge of Lieuts. Ellsworth, of Co. F., and Wilkie, of Co. G., for transfer to some veteran command. This detachment numbered one hundred and sixty-two enlisted men, and was subsequently assigned to the 47th Illinois Infantry. On the 28th day of July, transportation being in readiness, the regiment embarked at Montgomery, on the small steamers "Red Chief" and "Coquette," and proceeded down the Alabama river to Selma, where it arrived on the following morning. Disembarking here, it proceeded thence by railroad through Demopolis and Meridian, to Jackson, Miss., reaching this point July 31st. The railroad between Jackson and Vicksburg having been thoroughly destroyed by the Federal armies during the campaign against the latter place, had not been repaired, and the regiment was obliged to march from Jackson to the Big Black, a distance of about forty miles. It started from Jackson on the evening of August 1st, and came out ten miles to Clinton, where it camped at 11 o'clock P. M. Resuming the march early on the following morning, the regiment moved forward August 2nd, twenty-two miles, over the old battle-fields at Champion Hills, and camped the same night within a short distance of the Big Black bridge. It took the cars at this place in the afternoon of the 3rd, and arrived at Vicksburg safely that evening. It was expected the command would remain at this rendezvous, and be mustered out of the service before being sent to the State for final payment. Such orders were received from Maj. Gen. Smith, by the regimental commander on leaving Montgomery, but Maj. Gen. Slocum, in command at Vicksburg, deeming it for the interest of the Government to send the troops immediately up the river, ordered the Ninety-fifth to proceed to St. Louis, Mo., and report to the chief mustering officer at that post for muster-out. The regiment accordingly embarked at Vicksburg, August 5th, on the steamer "Mollie Able," and after a pleasant trip up the Mississippi, arrived at St. Louis on the 10th. It did not remain here, however, to muster out, and soon received orders from Maj. Gen. Pope, commanding the Department of Missouri, to proceed to Springfield, Ill., for final payment and discharge from the service.

The organization reached Springfield, August 11th,

on a common freight train, generously provided for the occasion, was enthusiastically received at the dêpot by a delegation of Jewish clothing merchants, and after paying for its own transportation on the cars from the city to "Camp Butler," was assigned good quarters in the barracks at that encampment.

The company commanders now applied themselves diligently, day and night, to the completion of the muster-out rolls, which had been begun at Montgomery. This was a lengthy and tedious work for them, as several of these rolls had to be made out, in which it was necessary to properly account for all men who had ever belonged to the organization, and give an accurate report of their pay, clothing, and other accounts with the Government; also blank discharges were filled up and furnished to each soldier mustered out with the command.

Through extraordinary efforts on the part of the officers, all the necessary papers for final discharge were completed by the 15th of August, pronounced perfect by the mustering officer, and on the day following, the regiment was formally mustered out of the United States service by Captain James A. Hall, of the 1st U. S. Cavalry.

On the 21st day of August the officers and enlisted men received full and final payment, and in a body left Springfield the same evening on a special train for Chicago, and their respective homes. Preparations had been made in the counties where the regiment was raised, to give the various companies appropriate receptions on their arrival, and delegations were sent to meet the regiment at Chicago. Hon. Allen C. Fuller was present, and escorted the Boone county companies to Belvidere, where a large concourse of people greeted the returning veterans, and with fitting and patriotic ceremonies welcomed them back to their homes from the war. The several companies from McHenry county were received with similar demonstrations, in the various localities to which they returned.

Here closes the military career of the regiment. While the surviving members point with pride to its record during the war, and rejoice in its instrumentality in crushing the rebellion and securing the triumph of the National cause, yet it is to be remembered with sadness, that all these grand results were accomplished only at the expense and sacrifice of valuable life and limb.

Out of the aggregate nine hundred and eighty-three officers and enlisted men, who originally accompanied the regiment to the field, only about half of them returned and mustered out with the organization. One hundred and ninety men were discharged during the service, mostly for disabilities incurred after leaving their homes. Many of these returned to their friends, pale, haggard, and broken down by the sufferings and diseases incident to camp life. But in looking over the record of the regiment, the most sorrowful recollection of all is, that eighty-three of our noble comrades laid down their lives while filling their places of duty on the battle-field, and died of wounds received in action, while one hundred and seventy-seven became the pitiful victims of disease, and from this cause closed their earthly career while in the service of their country.

Long is the list of our fallen companions, our valorous and patriotic dead; they shine forth in our regimental history as valiant heroes who offered their own lives, willing sacrifices upon the altar of their country, that rebellion might perish, and the nation's life be preserved.

Their deeds and virtues will ever be treasured well in memory by the survivors of the regiment, and the dependent ones whom they may have left behind will be remembered and cared for by a deeply sympathizing, generous and patriotic public.

APPENDIX.

ROSTER OF COMMISSIONED OFFICERS AND NON-COMMISSIONED STAFF,
SHOWING
Muster-in, Resignations, Deaths and Promotions during Service.

FIELD AND STAFF.

Col. LAWRENCE S. CHURCH; appointed Aug. 22, 1862; mustered into U. S. service Sept. 4, 1862, date of muster-in of the regiment; resignation accepted Jan. 24, 1863.

Col. THOS. W. HUMPHREY; appointed Lieut. Colonel Aug. 22, 1862; mustered in Sept. 4, 1862; promoted Colonel May 21, 1863, to rank from Jan. 24, 1863; killed in action at Guntown June 10, 1864. Brevetted Brigadier General.

Col. LEANDER BLANDEN; appointed Major Aug. 22, 1862; mustered in Sept. 4, 1862; promoted to Lieut. Colonel May 21, 1863, to rank from Jan. 24, 1863; promoted to Colonel Oct. 13, 1864, to rank from Sept. 1, 1864.

Lieut. Col. WM. AVERY; promoted to Major from Captain Co. "A," May 21, 1863; promoted to Lieut. Colonel Nov. 16, 1864.

Major CHARLES B. LOOP; promoted to Major from Captain Co. "B," Oct. 16, 1864.

Adjt. WALES W. WOOD; appointed Aug. 26, 1862; mustered in Sept. 4, 1862.

Quartermaster HENRY D. BATES; mustered in Sept. 4, 1862; resigned March 29, 1863.

Quartermaster GARDNER S. SOUTHWORTH; promoted from First Lieut. Co. "I," May 14, 1863.

Surgeon George N. Woodward; appointed Oct. 10, 1862; resigned March 24, 1863.

Surgeon John W. Green; appointed April 24, 1863; mustered in May 6, 1863.

Asst. Surgeon Walter F. Suiter; appointed Oct. 7, 1862; mustered in Oct. 21, 1862.

Asst. Surgeon Ansel D. Merritt; appointed Oct. 28, 1862; resigned March 24, 1863.

Asst. Surgeon Josiah Giddings; appointed April 30, 1863; mustered in May 13, 1863.

Chaplain Thos. R. Satterfield; appointed Oct. 9, 1862; mustered in same date; resigned June 9, 1864.

Chaplain Jas. H. More; appointed Sept. 16, 1864; mustered in same date.

NON-COMMISSIONED STAFF.

Sergt. Major Bennett T. Wakeman; appointed at organization of regiment; discharged from service March 18, 1863, for disability.

Sergt. Major Milo S. Brown; promoted from the ranks Aug. 7, 1863; died of disease at Memphis, Tenn., July 7, 1864.

Sergt. Major Mark Hathaway; promoted from Co. "H," April 2, 1863; discharged to receive promotion April 26, 1863.

Sergt. Major Charley Curtis; promoted from Co. "B," July 7, 1863.

Q. M. Sergt. Wm. H. Earley; appointed and mustered in at organization of regiment.

Com. Sergt. John H. Hurlbut; appointed and mustered in with regiment; returned to Co. "F" for duty, June 1, 1863.

Com. Sergt. Franklin H. Bosworth; promoted from the ranks June 1, 1863.

Hosp. Steward Wilbur P. Buck; appointed at organization of regiment; discharged for promotion as Asst. Surgeon in 17th Illinois Infantry, Jan. 18, 1864.

Hosp. Steward John W. Groesbeck; promoted from

the ranks Jan. 18, 1864; discharged for promotion as Asst. Surgeon in 81st Illinois Infantry, Dec. 6, 1864.

Hosp. Steward FRANCIS P. DICKINSON; promoted from the ranks Dec. 6, 1864.

Drum Major THEODORE INGHAM, and Fife Major JUSTUS M. SHEFFIELD; appointed and mustered in at organization of regiment; discharged (being in excess of organization,) March 2, 1863.

Principal Musicians ALMIRON T. VANLEUVEN and PETER WHITE; promoted from the ranks, May 1st, 1863.

LINE OFFICERS.

COMPANY "A."

Captain ALEX. S. STEWART, mustered in as First Lieut. Sept. 4, 1862; promoted to Captain May 21, 1863.

First Lieut. JAS. E. SPONABLE; mustered in as Second Lieut. Sept. 4, 1862; promoted to First Lieutenancy May 21, 1863; died of wounds received at Vicksburg, Miss., May 22, 1863.

First Lieut. JOHN B. BABCOCK; promoted from Sergt. to Second Lieut. May 21, 1863; promoted to First Lieut; resigned.

First Lieut. AMOS J. BOYINGTON; promoted from Sergt. to Second Lieut.; promoted to First Lieut. June 23, 1863.

Second Lieut. BENJAMIN F. PARKER; promoted from Sergt. to Second Lieut. June 23, 1863.

COMPANY "B."

Captain JAMES M. TISDEL; promoted from Sergt. to Second Lieut. Jan. 1, 1864; from Second Lieut. to First Lieut. April, 1864; from First Lieut. to Captain Oct. 10, 1864.

First Lieut. MILTON E. KEELER; mustered in Sept. 4, 1862; resigned.

First Lieut. WM. H. H. CURTIS; promoted to Second Lieut. from Sergt.; promoted to First Lieut. Oct. 16, 1864.

Second Lieut. AARON F. RANDALL; mustered in Sept. 4, 1862; resigned Jan. 16, 1863.

Second Lieut. EDWARD PIERCE; promoted from Sergt. to Second Lieut.; resigned July 26, 1863.

Second Lieut. EDWARD H. ROSECRANS; promoted from Sergt. to Second Lieut. Oct. 16, 1864.

COMPANY "C."

Capt. JASON B. MANZER; mustered in Sept. 4, 1862; killed in action at Vicksburg, Miss., May 22, 1863.

Capt. OTIS H. SMITH; mustered in as Second Lieut. Sept. 4, 1862; promoted to Captain July 10, 1863.

First Lieut. WM. W. WEDGEWOOD; mustered in Sept. 4, 1862; mustered out Dec. 31, 1862.

First Lieut. PHILIAR L. WELLS; promoted from Sergt. to Second Lieut. March 26, 1863; promoted to First Lieut. July 10, 1863.

Second Lieut. SAMUEL CUTTER; promoted from Sergt. to Second Lieut. July 10, 1863.

COMPANY "D."

Capt. EDWARD J. COOK; mustered in Sept. 4, 1862; died of wounds received in action at Vicksburg, May 22, 1863.

Capt. JOHN E. BECKLEY; mustered in as First Lieut. Sept. 4, 1862; promoted to Captain Aug. 19, 1863.

First Lieut. WM. H. HUFFMAN; mustered in as Second Lieut. Sept. 4, 1862; promoted to First Lieut. Aug. 19, 1863.

Second Lieut. JAMES CASLER; promoted to Second Lieut. from Sergt. Aug. 8, 1864.

COMPANY "E."

Capt. JOHN EDDY; mustered in Sept. 4, 1862.

First Lieut. ASA FARNUM; mustered in Sept. 4, 1862; dismissed the service Sept. 24, 1864; reinstated.

Second Lieut. OSCAR E. DOWE, mustered into service Sept. 4, 1862; resigned March 25, 1863.

Second Lieut. THOS. GILKERSON; promoted to Second Lieut. from Sergt. June 1, 1863; resigned Dec. 11, 1864.

Second Lieut. ALBERT J. ALDERMAN; promoted to Second Lieut. from Sergt. Oct. 16, 1864.

COMPANY "F."

Capt. WM. H. STEWART; mustered in Sept. 4, 1862.

First Lieut. SABINE VAN CUREN; mustered in Sept. 4, 1862; resigned May 26, 1863.

First Lieut. MAURICE F. ELLSWORTH; promoted from Sergt. to Second Lieut.; from Second to First Lieut. July 10, 1863.

Second Lieut. PHINEAS H. KERR; mustered in Sept. 4, 1862; resigned Feb. 22, 1863.

Second Lieut. JAS. MORROW; mustered in ——; resigned Sept. 8, 1864.

Second Lieut. GEO. ECKERT; appointed Aug. 1865, (not mustered.)

COMPANY "G."

Capt. ELLIOTT N. BUSH; mustered in Sept. 4, 1862; killed in action at Guntown June 10, 1864.

Capt. HENRY M. BUSH; promoted from First Lieut. to Captain Oct. 17, 1864.

First Lieut. JEREMIAH WILCOX; promoted to Second Lieut. from Sergt.; promoted to First Lieut. Dec. 25, 1864.

Second Lieut. W. W. WOOD; promoted to Adjt. Aug. 26, 1862.

Second Lieut. JOSEPH M. COLLYER; mustered in Sept. 4, 1862; died of disease June 24, 1863.

Second Lieut. CHARLES W. IVES; promoted from Sergt. to Second Lieut. June 24, 1863; resigned Sept. 8, 1864.

Second Lieut. DAVID WILKIE; promoted from Sergt. to Second Lieut. Dec. 25, 1864.

COMPANY "H."

Captain CHAS. H. TRYON; mustered in Sept. 4, 1862; resigned Feb. 18, 1863.

Capt. JAS. H. WETMORE, promoted from First Lieut. to Captain July 1, 1864.

First Lieut. WM. B. WALKER; promoted from Second Lieut. to First Lieut. July 1, 1863.

Second Lieut. JOHN P. RANSOM; promoted from Sergt. to Second Lieut. July 1, 1863.

COMPANY "I."

Capt. JAS. NISH; mustered in Sept. 4, 1862.

First Lieut. THOS. H. JACKSON; promoted from Sergt. to First Lieut. May 29, 1863; died of wounds received in action at Guntown, June 10, 1864.

First Lieut. WM. H. IDE; promoted from Sergt. to First Lieut. Aug. 1, 1864.

Second Lieut. CONVERSE PIERCE; mustered in Sept. 4, 1862; resigned.

Second Lieut. ASA L. WEAVER; promoted from Sergt. to Second Lieut.

COMPANY "K."

Capt. GABRIEL E. CORNWELL; mustered in Sept. 4, 1862; killed in action at Vicksburg, Miss., May 22, 1863.

Capt. ALMON SCHELLENGER; promoted from First Lieut. to Captain July 10, 1863.

First Lieut. ALONZO BROOKS; promoted from Second Lieut. to First Lieut. July 10, 1863.

Second Lieut. JOHN D. ABBE; promoted from Sergt. to Second Lieut. July 10, 1863; resignation accepted Sept. 19, 1864.

Second Lieut. ALFRED D. CHENEY; promoted from Sergt. to Second Lieut. Feb. 15, 1865.

LIST SHOWING COMMISSIONED OFFICERS AND ENLISTED MEN

Mustered out with Regiment, Transferred, Discharged, Died and Deserted.

A * is placed after the names of the officers and men who were not mustered out with the regiment, but discharged elsewhere.

FIELD AND STAFF, AND NON-COMMISSIONED STAFF.

Mustered out with Regiment.

Col. Leander Blanden, Lieut. Col. Wm. Avery, Major Charles B. Loop, Adjt. W. W. Wood, Surgeon John W.

Green, Asst. Surgeon Walter F. Suiter, Asst. Surgeon Josiah Giddings, Quartermaster Gardner S. Southworth, Chaplain James H. More; Sergeant Major Charley Curtis, Quartermaster Sergeant Wm. H. Earley, Commissary Sergeant Franklin H. Bosworth, Hospital Steward Francis P. Dickinson, Principal Musicians, Almiron T. Vanleuven and Peter White.

COMPANY "A."
Mustered out with Regiment.

Captain Alexander S. Stewart, *First Lieutenant* Amos J. Boyington, *Second Lieutenant* Benj. T. Parker.

Sergeants Henry M. Fillmore, George W. Sponable, Wm. H. Sanders, Calvin G. Handy,* John Kennedy.*

Corporals Lafayette Wands, Dennis S. Jones, Lewis Gray, Joseph Schneider, Robt. Crinklaw, Henry P. Crane, Clark J. Hogeboom, Wilford Mallory.

Privates Alexander O. Adams, Wm. M. Benjamin, John H. Beam, Jas. H. Bogardus, Wm. H. Babcock,* Orrin R. Clark,* Titus R. DeWolf, Frederick Diggins, Saml. Ellis, Henry H. Felt, Peter Groat, Alonzo. B. Graves, Elias J. Goodrich, Dexter Hall, John Howard, John H. Howard, Wm. M. Hamilton, Silas A. Hardy, Almeron Herrick, Wm. H. Jones, Henry E. Knapp, Coe Kilgore, Warren W. Langdon, John W. Langdon, Wilbur F. Morris,* Hiram Morris,* Dan'l W. Mitchell, Nelson Noble, George H. Onthank, Patrick O'Brien, Horace Plumb, Rich'd Pillion, Felix Reamer, George Styers, Alexander Smith,* Nelson F. Shearer, Edwin E. Sponable, Wm. C. Sullivan, James A. Tracy, George Townsend, Charles S. Trowbridge,* Henry Trebelock, Samuel Trebelock, James Thatcher, Dan'l W. Webb, Harrison Wing, Samuel Welsh; Madison Monroe (under cook of A. D.)

Transferred.

Wilbur P. Buck, to non-commissioned staff as Hospital Steward, Corporal Milo S. Brown, promoted Sergt. Major.

Privates Wm. J. Casley, Christopher Conley, Jeremiah Devine, to V. R. C., Wm. Farnum, Guy F. Goodman, Theodore Ham, Dan'l Hazen, Geo. W. Hamilton, Aruna Holbrook, Orren Hubbard, Henry Hilflicker, Natt Huff, Parley Inman, Frank Lam, Emery Ladd, Russell Mallory, Edward McMullen, James O'Brien, Henry H. Paynter, George R. Paynter, Luther Pomeroy, Silas H. Roy, Job Robbins, Jas. H. Smith, Obadiah Sands, Joseph Tormy, George Thompson, Jas. Terrill, John Wallace, Almiron T. Vanleuven.

Discharged.

Privates Fayette H. Ball, Sam'l H. Ball, Ezra C. Bedford, Nathan C. Barlow, Albert Drake, John B. Fletcher, Neil S. Graves, Byman T. Henry, Justus R. Henry, Bailey S. Hart, Andrew J. Jones, John Maher, Joseph Metcalf, Jas. Madden, Smith W. Nolen, Isaac Newell, Robt. P. Roy, Samuel R. Pettingale, Samuel Rowland, Charles H. Tucker, Wm. Wylie, Merritt H. Wright.

Died.

Corporals Curtis Fuller and Joseph Timony.
Privates Elijah Bent, Jas. Cornes, John C. Cook, Augustus J. Fletcher, Andrew Gamble, Sidney R. Heath, Derias Howe, Elijah Lyons, Libbeus Olcott, Michael P. O'Neal, Christopher Rourke, James F. Smith, Frank Shores, Robt. G. Smith, John Starks, George W. Smith, Samuel Snyder, Clark P. Thompson, James G. Williams, Thomas Welsh, Wm. F. Wallace.

Deserted.

Privates Charles Magrath, Wm. Campbell, Thos. Smith; George Adams (under cook of A. D.)

COMPANY "B."

Mustered out with Regiment.

Captain James M. Tisdel, *First Lieutenant* Wm. H. H. Curtis, *Second Lieutenant* Edward H. Rosecrans.

Sergeants Henry B. Bogardus, Charles W. Webb, Joseph Sweetapple, Wm. Heflin, John G. Morley.

Corporals Wm. R. Stevenson, Charles A. Studley, Paul

Hostrawser, Robt. Ridge, Wm. F. Hill, Smith T. Marvin, Harvey Smith, Wm. B. Chilvers.

Privates Julius C. Bishop, George Blatchford, George Barnes, John Butler, Henry A. Chambers, Charles Church, Daniel Chamberlain, Gilbert B. Carpenter, Alexander S. Cummings, John Collier, Lemuel Demerest, Richard Delany, Jeremiah Fitz Maurice, James G. Goodman,* Andrew Galagher, Austin Hovey, Francis T. Houk, Thomas D. Horton, Alfred M. Horton, Oscar F. Herren, Ira D. Hill, Walter Harder, Wellington Harder, Orlando Loper,* Harmon McCoy, Henry J. Munzer, Thomas Moore, John J. Merrill, John Martin, Frederick Morley, John Moore, David A. Moore,* Joseph Nutall, James O. Donnell, Edwin E. E. Park, Mortimer L. Powell,* George W. Sackett, Sylvester L. Stevenson, Elias Shockley, Alvin M. Smith, Henry Shattleman, George Spencer, Ransom Thompson, Joseph D. Tibbits, Dan'l G. Winegar, George W. Winegar, Wm. N. Tyler.*

Transferred.

Privates Wm. Barr, Smith Collar, Francis H. Curtis, Garrett Dupuy, Lawrence Fagan, Thore Johnson, John Johnson, Jeremiah A. Jacobs, Chester C. Leach, James Murphey, John H. Parsons, John H. Searl, Timothy Sergeant, George F. Tongue, Peter White (promoted to principal musician), Wm. O. Newcomb, Charles Curtis (promoted to Sergt. Major.)

Discharged.

Corporals Solomon H. Bailey, Chas. B. Drake.

Privates Isaac Conner, Peter Cramer, Hiram Draper, George Marvin, Osborn Allen, Edward Barker, George H. Griffin, Elisha J. Leach, Robert Atkinson, James R. Manning, Washington Porter, Mervin Andrews, David Cox, Albert C. Haight, David E. Marvin.

Died.

Sergeants Charles Anderson, Albert E. Locke, Stephen A. Rollins.

Corporal John Horan.

Privates Wm. H. Boyce, John Corcoran, Martin Dixon, Benjamin Easton, Charles Farnsworth, Wm. H. Mead, Jas. C. Miller, Wm. McNally, Kittel Mikkleson, John Randolph, Wm. E. Shepardson, Albert W. Seibert, David F. Studley, John Sexton, Ephraim A. Tyler, Job H. Westbury, Henry Williams, Edwin Hovey, Elisha N. Strong.

Deserted.

Privates Thomas Kelley, Albert D. Carpenter; David Seams, Gideon Boddis, and Thomas Crawford (under cooks of A. D.)

COMPANY "C."

Mustered out with Regiment.

Captain Otis H. Smith, *First Lieutenant* Philiar L. Wells, *Second Lieutenant* Samuel Cutter.

Sergeants George W. Reynolds, Stillman Hills, Alfred Bell, Murray E. Randall, Darius C. Kingsbury.

Corporals Abijah T. Conklin, Everill J. Hills, Randolph E. Slawson, Wesley D. Miner, Wm. Gerrett, Joshua Cross, Dwight F. Allison, Wm. H. Gray.

Privates Chas. R. Andrews, Robert L. Burns,* Frederick Butikofer, Wm. Burton, Robt. Buchanan, Patrick Barrett, Jerome Bailey, Alpheus Cook, Chas. Chilson,* Wm. H. Chilson, Sam'l Cole, Sam'l A. Dunham,* Geo. B. Dunham,* Chas. H. Downs, Byron Degraw, Geo. S. Fradenburgh, Joseph Groskinsky, Jos. Gay, Valentine K. M. Groesbeck, Francis D. Garnsey, Theodore W. Goodsell, Nathan W. Gary, Willmoth Gillis, Orrin F. Hutchinson, Marcus A. Hubell, Patrick Hoey,* Isaac Harris,* Alfred Hawver, Chas. Hawver, John W. King, George King, Patrick Keeler, Augustus Labrec, John Listickow, Chas. Mosher, Chas. H. Parkhurst,* Schuyler J. Piersons, Brookins A. Plummer, Edgar F. Reed,* John M. Smith, Horace L. Scott, Newel Seeley, Willard J. Scott, John O. Stevens, Benjamin N. Smith,* Chas. J. Toby, Asad Udell, Riley Wheeler, Edwin E. Winney, Robert Wheeler, Henry Wheeler, Marcus Williamson; Stephen Jones and Lem Cupid (under cooks of A. D.)

ILLINOIS INFANTRY VOLUNTEERS.

Transferred.

Privates Daniel S. Cummings, Thos. L. Dixon, George F. Downs, John O. Flinn, John W. Groesbeck, Wm. Hollister, Byron A. Howe, James Jewell, Peter Keenan, Henry E. Mose, Waterman Merry, James A. Piersons, Garrett Perforso, James N. Reynolds, Sherman Rector, Wm. P. Riley, Wm. H. Rector, Joseph H. Scott, James Tulip, Dolphus Vanslyke, Bennett T. Wakeman (promoted to Sergt. Major, afterwards transferred as recruit.)

Discharged.

Sergeants Chas. Armstrong, Sam'l S. Sergeant.

Corporals Thomas J. Disbrow, Chas. B. Dodge, Ichabod M. Meeker, Alonzo Wakeman.

Privates Ezra C. Burton, Damon W. Davis, George A. Fish, Henry La Brec, Mahlon Piper, Edwin Rector, Adelbert Russell, Theodore Rebadero, Smith B. Tooker, James Tulip, Jr.

Died.

Sergeant Wm. H. Stoddard.

Corporals Charles Bigsby, Jonas Stevens.

Privates Alfred Ayres, Wm. Brown, Dan'l S. Broughton, Edwin Bellows, Seely Brown, Henry Bills, Thomas J. Brown, Wm. C. Branden, Reuben Cook, Lewis Deno, John G. DeGroat, Edgar I Dodge, George W. Dixon, Nelson Helm, Levi Harp, Sam'l H. Jackson, Victor La Brec, David D. Lake, William Marshall, Andrew A. McCorn, Marion Pease, Ira M. Pearce, Alfred D. Randall, Wm. Shult, Jason W. Smith, Wm. W. Stetler, Alexander Snow, Hiram Scott, Wm. Tooker, Henry Vandeusen, James Venard, George P. Wetlaufer, John H. Wheeler, John Wentworth, Adam Wetlaufer.

Deserted — *Privates* John M. Hunt, Morton B. Kasson.

COMPANY "D."

Mustered out with Regiment.

Captain John E. Beckley, *First Lieutenant* Wm. H. Huffman, *Second Lieutenant* James Casler.

Sergeants Onley L. Andrews, Julius E. Baker, Martin D. Kellogg, Sam'l Foster, James Kittle.

Corporals Alfred Morse, Dwight B. Warner, John H. Doran, John Powers, Alonzo Paris, Chauncey D. Parker, Daniel E. Newcomb, Carlos DeGoff.

Privates Henry Arndt, Henry C. Bywater,* Wm. Butler, Chas. Booth, John G. Church,* Albert W. Coats, Wm. Diamond,* Lloyd J. Davis, Henry R. Dunton,* Frank Gennett, Nelson Gates, Anson D. Hopkins,* Herman Hiderman, Roderick Hodge, August Kappie, George H. Kam,* Thos. Leggett, Richard Lawless, Wm. Mulock, Geo. W. Morris, Thos. McFadden, John Nelson,* Wm. H. Noyes, Geo. Nugent, Thos. Powers, Thos. Peacock, Wm. Peacock, Daniel W. Richardson,* Henry M. Shannon, Geo. Swindell,* Henry Scalan, Joseph Slater, Theodore H. Sedgwick, Wm. Smallwood, Chas. Willey, Jas. Wallace, Hinton Wheeler.

Transferred.

Privates Eaton P. Blaisdell, Lyman Bacon, Horace Butterfield, Henry W. Beardsley, Wm. Dickerson, Sam'l H. Drew, Frederick H. Foster, Wm. B. Fry, Mark Goodhand, Geo. A. Hoeg, Wm. Jones, Chas. W. Long, Wm. Mullen, Jas. McDavis, Frank Manore, Jas. F. Packer, Francis Rollow, Mark Rebel, Wilson Turner, Stanton D. Warner.

Discharged.

Sergeants Hiram M. Bryant, Jas. Casler, Frederick Leyman.

Corporal Stanton D. Warner.

Privates Henry W. Beardsley, Henry J. Chittenden, Edson J. Davis, George E. Dunn, Andrew Henderson, Bennett Hicks, John L. Keller, John Leggett, Miron L Lee, John G. Mauney, Milton McCollum, Philip L. Melius, Able W. Noyes, Jas. L. Payne, Jas. W. Powers, Jas. W. Ryan, Wm. H. Rotnour, Wm. St. Clair, Wm. S. Shales, John Tromblee, Abram Vanbogart, Cornelius Vanbogart, Orlando Vanbogart, Wm. A. Wright, Wm. H. Cook, John Keepsill.

Died.

Sergeant Chas. C. Barnes.
Corporals Enos H. Barnes, Chas. W. Foster, Phillip R. Morris, Paul Shawl, Emer Nallen, Thos. McLean.
Privates John Booth, Alonzo D. Crocker, Charles H. Francisco, Thos Fitzsimmons, Jas. Fleming, Andrew Huff, Joseph Hutson, David Housel, Carl Leher, Wm. R. Miller, Andrew Olson, Chas. H. Paine, Richard Taylor, Elijah P. Weaver, Levi Waterman, Isaac Wescot; Scip. Weatherford (under cook of A. D.)

Deserted.

Privates Wm. G. Gleason, Lewis Medock, John Tromblee.

COMPANY "E."

Mustered out with Regiment.

Captain John Eddy, *First Lieutenant* Asa Farnum,* *Second Lieutenant* Albert J. Alderman.
Sergeants William Andrews, Edwin R. Morris, Clark Rogers, Frederick Maushak, George V. Barnard.
Corporals Patrick H. Kennedy, Andrew Fern, James Stevenson, Thomas Cohill, George W. Miller, Amos Capron, David S. Marshall.
Privates John D. Atwater, Dwight Andrus, Henry Andrus, Oscar Andrus,* John Alexander, Chas. Burton, Chas. Ballard, Joseph Brown, Delo Bunnell, John W. Burnside,* James Barry, McKendee F. Bishop, George G. Blake, Chas. S. Blakesley, Peter Breen, Frank G. Ball,* Darwin Barrows, Dexter S. Cowles, George Cline, Robert Cummings,* Fuller V. Colver, Nathaniel Colver, Guiles M. Durkee, John David, Andrew Farrell, John Flemming, Luther D. Fillmore, Woodberry Hardy, Chas. A. Holden, Aaron Howard, Andrew P. Howard, John P. Jewett, Ezra O. Knapp, John C. Lightner, David Little, John J. Mosser, Ephraim A. Marsh, John Murphy, Girnri S. Molton, Romanzo Moore, Francis H. Nickles, Porter B. Nickles,* Samuel L. A. Patchin, Joseph A. Ross, William Swart, Andrew W. Sears,* Ward B. Smith,* James Stott, Jacob

Vrooman, Joseph Weaver, Albert Wheelon, Frederick E. Woodward, Ira Webber, James White, Nathaniel White, Joseph G. Young.

Transferred.

Corporals Chauncey G. Wait, Moses C. Fitzer.

Privates John H. Brown, Allison C. Bulard, Patrick Breen, Lawrence Breen, Richard Brown, Henry Bright, Norman Clapp, Thomas Corcoran, Jas. Carroll, Richard Cahill, Wm. Day, Ashael Eddy, Henry C. Eddy, Illot G. Gillot, Wm. H. Glass, Thomas Holliday, Justus Knapp, Linus F. Larkins, George D Lillie, John Jobe, Thomas Robinson, Charles C. Reynolds, Newell D. Sanford, Merrit C. Stoddard, Wm. Thompson, Israel Wood.

Discharged.

Sergeants John Prowse, Frank M. Jewett.

Corporal Jas. Stott.

Privates Wm. H. Ballard, Francis H. Burnside, Clark Bulard, Clark A. Beebe, Edgar Bowen, John E. Best, Wm. H. Brown, Uriah L. Colgrove, Uri Farr, Sanford Hardy, John Hatch, Henry Jobe, Chas. Morgan, Marcus L. Olmstead, Daniel Piper, Daniel A. Steadman, William F. Smith, John J. W. Starr, Ahira Thompson, Jas. Tuley, Jacob Vedder.

Died.

Privates John L. Alderman, Jas. Best, William Bassett, George Bassett, George Barrows, David Beck, Turner Calkins, Wesley J. Colgrove, Jas. B. Delamater, Clark Everest, Levi F. Fitzer, Jas. Kennedy, Jas. McEwen Lee, Samuel Mullis, Henry Maddick, George Miller, Carlos J. Morse, Elias H. Nettleton, John W. Oaks, Martin Perry, Richard Prowse, Hiram Stevens, Elisha H. Higley (missing, and supposed dead); Henry Kelley (under cook of A. D.)

Deserted.

Privates George Hald, Jacob Myer; Aaron Janes (under cook of A. D.)

COMPANY "F."

Mustered out with Regiment.

Captain Wm. H. Stewart, *First Lieutenant* M. F. Ellsworth,* *Second Lieutenant* George Eckert.

Sergeants Frederick D. Snyder, Rufus Thompson,* Alex. Hunter, Joseph Roden.

Corporals Allen Giles, Edgar Fox, Patrick H. Walsh, Martin Tiffany, Dewitt C. McCrary, Egbert Fox, Peter Zimmer, Andrew Oleson.

Privates Franklin Alvord, George R. Bassett, Linus E. Boomer, Thos. Blakeslee, Milo Churchill, Theodore Chambers, Henry W. Chase, Barney Etten, Ezra Fox,* Milon Fosdick, Hiram R. Grey, Oscar Hickox, Jacob Kohn, John Lutzen, Nicholas Myer, Patrick McNeemy, Wm. C. Neale, Peet Overton, Michael Powers, Azariah Rider, Thos. Sutton, John Stampp, Jas. Smith, Walter Thompson,* Dewey Thompson,* Alexander Tweed, Clark Waterman, Luman C. Wheelock, Peter G. Weitzel; Sam'l Austin and Dick Hilliard (under cooks of A. D.)

Transferred.

Privates Silas Baker, John Barrett, Morris F. Brown, Francis P. Dickinson, Robt. Feely, Thomas Glennore, John H. King, Joseph Lester, Thos. Lindsey, Alanson O. Moore, Peter Munro, Patrick O'Brien, George B. Wiltshire.

Discharged.

Corporal Wm. P. Phelon.

Privates Adelbert Albright, Lewis Ballard, Jonathan W. Covey, Wm. J. Daily, Chas. L. Ellsworth, Aretus K. Field, John B. Hulbert, Alfred Hues, Albert Hayward, Edward E. Lawless, Wm. H. H. Lawless, Geo. W. Parsons, Morris J. Parks, Wm. A. Parker, Benjamin B. Reynolds, John B. Sanford, Justus M. Sheffield, Cyrus Wheelock.

Died.

Sergeant James Tibbetts.

Privates Wm. A. Churchill, Joseph H. Cooper, Joseph Cutforth, Geo. W. French, Darius W. Green, Peter J.

Haggerty, Henry Hess, Henry E. Hicks, Wm. Jacobs, Henry L. Kerr, Patrick Kelly, Hubert Mertz, Archibald Marshall, Nelson Martin, George W. Nichols, Sylvester M. Paddock, Oliver E. Pomeroy, Dan'l W. Ryan, Alonzo C. Swan, Thos. Skillicorn, Chas. Sutton, Chas. Stevers, George Lawyer, John Sullivan, Jas. Tibbetts, Josiah Tuttle, John W. Vasey.

Deserted.

Privates Charles H. Cornish, Frank Hardin, Lorenzo Parker, Jas. M. Sheffield, John Walter.

COMPANY "G."
Mustered out with Regiment.

Captain Henry M. Bush, *First Lieutenant* Jeremiah Wilcox, *Second Lieutenant* David Wilkie.*

Sergeants Daniel B. Cornell,* Dwight S. Gookins, Geo. M. Bell, Benson B. Arbunckle, Wm. Gilkerson.*

Corporals Wells Briggs,* John M. Smith, Marcus R. Abbott, James S. Robbins, Edward L. Foot, Robt. Horan, Thomas Hannah, Jr.

Privates John Allen, Peter Ashland,* Orrin Barnes, Geo. L. Bennett, Albert Blood, Eli Brainard, Nathan L. Bristol, Henry M. Bacon, Albert D. J. Cashier, Hawley A. Caswell,* Charles Danforth, John H. Dible, Benj. F. Eastman, Hawley Feakins, Wm. H. Frederick, Parker T. Gibbs, Charles H. Gleason, Buel F. Hanks, John M. Hogan, Shirley A. Johnson, Darwin E. Keeler,* Eber Lucas, Joseph E. McCormick, Jay H. Morton, J. Adderly Moore, John Morrison,* Charles C. Mullen, Amos Norton, Henry O'Neil, George A. Oaks, Orris C. Peebles, Samuel Pepper, Wm. P. Perry, Richard D. Pierce, John Ramsey,* Henry Riley, Washington Robb, Sylvester L. Russell, Joy H. Saxton,* Wm. M. Saum, Jacob Seibert,* Wm. L. Smith, Chas. P. Stocking,* Geo. W. Snow, Patrick F. Sughrue, Eugene H. Thomas, Daniel Weaver, Leslie Williams, Frederick Wood, Wm. Whitehead; Abram Boram (under cook of A. D.)

Transferred.

Privates James Conner, Willis Case, Lyman L. Downs,

Martin L. Field, John W. Houghtaling, David Milks, Sam'l W. Sweet, Jacob Stenner, Edgar Stafford, Peter Wise, Richard C. Wolverton.

Discharged.

Corporals Robert D. Hannah, Christopher N. Wilson.
Privates William Bryden, Peter Byron, John D. Caswell, David E. Chase, Henry F. Childs, George W. Downs, H. Ford Douglas, Charles Farnsworth, Wm. H. Garland, Pierce Gilbert, Wm. W. Hill, John Heckman, Edgar N. Lincoln, Luther A. Orcutt, Melvin A. Randall.

Died.

Sergeant James S. Collins.
Corporals Richard O. Gunn, Henry L. Potter, Almond Quackenboss.
Privates John E. Benedict, Charles Barnes, Royal Briggs, Charles O. Collins, Daniel W. Cahoon, Thomas Doran, Wm. H. Feakins, Wm. E. Gunn, Rufus B. Gile, Michael Hoyn, Warren Hamlin, Hiram Hudson, Horace C. Hakes, John Halloway, Arba Lankton, William Middleton, Josiah Orcutt, Carroll J. Pray, David F. Russell, Wm. Ray, Jr., Geo. E. Randall, James Wight, Andrew De Wolf.

Deserted.

Privates Joseph Ward, Wm. L. Borst; Wm. Gibson and Henry Boyd (under cooks of A. D.)

COMPANY "H."

Mustered out with Regiment.

Captain James H. Wetmore, *First Lieutenant* Wm. B. Walker, *Second Lieutenant* John P. Ransom.
Sergeants Charles W. Freeman, Nehemiah T. Moore,* Milton R. Goddard, Henry Freeman, Mathew W. Marten.
Corporals Wyman Wilson, Henry Waterman, Wallace J. Wilson, Eugene I. Thomas, Moses Frazier, Henry H. Rowe, Nathan H. Utter.
Privates John Q. Adams, John G. Bailey, John Bogart, George W. Bellknapp, Harrison Berry, Franklin Cole, Je-

rome Copeley, George Clark, Wm. W. Daniel, Joshua Diamond, Benjamin Fuller, Francis Gates, Wm. Gotbed, Jas. Gardner, John H. Holland,* Job Hathaway,* Gideon C. Hammer,* Samuel D. Porter, Willard D. Paine, Benjamin A. Parker, Sumner Sayles, John W. Sanborn, Authur A. Sheldon,* Rial Smith,* James Strain, Peter Strain,* Ernest D. Stilson, Charles L. Turner, Van Buren Truesdell, John Thompson, James Walsh, James Welch, Theodore E. Wainwright, Casper Wirfs, Gibson Wright; Benjamin Abbott, Wm. Dodd and Matthew Ferguson (under cooks of A.D.)

Transferred.

Privates George Barnard, Henry Barlow, John C. Becker, John N. Barbor, Lawrence D. Blackman, Martin Cole, Harvey C. Cowdry, James Duffy, John Eckert, John T. Groger, Lewis L. Galusha, James G. Graves, Jackson Hammers, Jeremiah Halderman, Wm. E. Hughes, Lucius J. Hobart, Theodore Ingham, Charles D. Judd, Charles E. Peterson, Marvel Pierce, Philo Roe, Patrick Roache, Wm. G. Tanner, Jacob Westerman, Caleb L. Williams.

Discharged.

Sergeants Mark Hathaway, Charles H. Hitchcock, Schuyler Marvin.

Corporal Wesley Scranton.

Privates Thomas Anderson, Albert B. Boone, George W. Bellknapp, Frederick Eppel, Charles C. Fay, Ira F. Fay, George T. Freeman, John B. Groat, Jackson Hammer, Henry Hart, John Hughes, Robert J. Kerle, Edward G. Kemball, Charles H. Merchant, Hartwell S. Meade, Amel Nibeck, Peter C. Riley, Charles Simmons, Moses Sawyer, Henry C. Swan, Charles Tesman, Wm. Wray, Benjamin Casey.

Died.

Sergeants Norman Baldwin, Richard D. Bailey.

Privates Lewis E. Gale, Willard Kimball, Benj. F. Springer, Julius Bultke, Watson Clary, John R. Erkenbreck, Thomas Ferguson, Horace Freeman, Collin Hughes, Olney King, Jas. N. Murphy, Thomas R. Meade, Irwin Porter, Thomas Rees, Clark R. Sanford, Fayette A. Thomas, Edgar Town, Spencer Ward.

ILLINOIS INFANTRY VOLUNTEERS.

Deserted.
Privates Richard Benneke, Doctor F. Cushman, Harmon Poppe, Henry Poppe.

COMPANY "I."
Mustered out with Regiment.

Captain James Nish, *First Lieutenant* Wm. H. Ide, *Second Lieutenant* Asa L. Weaver.

Sergeants Edwin Gilbert, Edwin R. Crabtree, Bemin K. Sparawk, Henry Van Camp, John W. Lockwood.

Corporals Jas. Kee, Jas. M. Allen, Jas. H. Van Camp, Alfred K. Nash, Warren W. Cady, Joseph C. Johnston, Vernon N. Ford, Francis Corkins.

Privates James W. Bethysen,* George W. Burgess, Wm. R. Burr, Alexander Bell, Marshall B. Brink,* Amos M. Bates, Oscar S. Crabtree, Patrick Crowley, Wm. P. Champlin, John Campbell,* Wm. B. Crane,* Levi A. Corkins, Justus Chapman,* Thomas M. Doyle, Isaac Edwards, David Edwards, Charles Edson,* Charles Gunderson, Wm. H. Goodenough, Austin Lindsey, George H. Makins, Napoleon B. Morrison, Wm. J. Miller, John Makins, Willard A. McNitt, Nathaniel Nish, Jas. O'Donoho, Dennis O'Day, Hezekiah P. Schuyler, David G. Shales, Benjamin B. Sheley, Isaac J. Smith, Franklin L. Smith,* John G. Smith, Isaac E. Wheeler, Wm. M. Wilcox, Samuel S. Crabtree, Davis Harris (missing in action.)

Transferred.
Privates Alonzo Andrews, Wm. C. Brown, Windfield S. Coss, Wm. Coss, Franklin E. Cox, John Larson, Alexander Nish, Daniel Alson, Patrick O'Brien, Charles H. Paddock, Elias G. Rhoades, Edward P. Slater, John Tiffany, Amos Wallace, Luzerne E. Warner, Wm. H. Earley, Franklin H. Bosworth, Truman Churchill, Orville E. Shely, John J. Adams, Horace B. Allen.

Discharged.
Sergeants John R. Church, Andrew M. Green.
Privates David Corbin, John H. Corl, Patrick Corkins, Addison D. Fowler, David Cummings, John F. Cary, Doras

Calkins, Andrew M. Green, John Hogan, Abram Hannas, George P. Keller, Christopher Kalahan, Henry Lindsey, John Morris, John Q. Miller, Noah H. Pratt, Sam'l T. Paddison, Stephen R. Pert, Edward P. Slater, Thompson Smock, John J. Schnyder, Adelbert A. Thomas, John R. Thompson, Abram Underkarr, Clark Weldon, Edwin Williams, Sylvester Lawson.

Died.

Sergeants George Titcomb.

Corporals Samuel E. Thomas, Charles F. Dodd, Bishop B. Pettibone, Charles W. Carpenter.

Privates Charles C. Cromwell, Ambrose B. Ford, Francis Geherke, Conrad Gotterman, David F. Huntley, Charles Loomis, Christopher Martin, Albert W. Torrence, Sam'l G. Vanhorn, Elijah B. Way, Thomas J. Wilcox, Wesley Wallace.

Deserted.

Privates Henry Alfing, Michael Gordon, John B. Haffy, Samuel Tibbetts.

COMPANY "K."

Mustered out with Regiment.

Captain Almon Schellenger, *First Lieutenant* Alonzo Brooks, *Second Lieutenant* Alfred D. Cheney.

Sergeants Sewell Vanalstine, John Vanantwerp, Henry Morgan, Joseph P. Smith, Joseph R. Lilley.

Corporals Laughlin Scougall, John T. Burrough,* Thos. W. Bowman, Gardner C. Wright, Stephen Dimond, Hans Stall.

Privates Cordenio Bruce,* Sam'l Bowman, Robt. Blake, John P. Coleman, Jas. Dymond,* John D. Dullam, James Ellis, Charles W. Fross, William Gibbs, Fredolen Geng,* Roswell Guile, Wm. Hutchins, Henry Hill,* Charles Kirk, Gideon B. Lewis, James Landon, Emery Lamel, Thomas Oleson, David Pichard,* Benj. B. Parks,* Henry B. Putnam, Wm. J. Rodawalt, Stephen Rodawalt, Henry M. Reser, Jay Renne, Wm. Reed, Joseph Sewell, George W. Streeter, Henry A. Streeter,* John H. Sitzer, Rufus Smith,

George W. Stockwell, James Vickers,* Thomas Vincent, Abner Wakefield, Leonard Wakefield, Philip P. Wheldon.

Transferred.

Privates Wm. H. Booth, John Desmore, George O. Elsworth, Eugene Elsworth, Jirald N. B. Joslin, Robt. Lafeaver, John R. Livingston, John G. Mansfield, John McCurtis, Thomas Muggins, Rufus Marks, Augustus Peck, Jas. Reed, Abraham Stockwell, George Shannon, James P. Smith, Olender A. Salisbury, Theodore Willson, Isaac Watts, Wm. Watts, A. Webster.

Discharged.

Corporals Wm. H. Chappell, Sam'l H. Hills.
Privates Martin Butler, Eli Burdick, Wm. A. Burdick, Hiram Barnes, Willard Hutchins, Roswell E. Hovey, Geo. E. Hanover, Alexander Klumph, Orson O. Miller, Horatio N. North, Nelson Oleson, Andrew Oleson, Robert Robinson, Aretemus Rolo, Henry Steele, Sam'l D. Sherman, Jas. B. Scougall, Thomas Shackle, Charles E. Sherman, Wm. H. Stockwell, Ira Smith, Henry Vanderwacker, Lewis W. E. Webster, Daniel Wakefield, Schuyler Wakefield.

Died.

Sergeants Joseph W. Bowman, Gabriel J. Cornwell.
Corporals Joseph N. Smith, Leland K. Green.
Privates John H. Atkinson, Henry S. Butterfield, Wm. T. Baker, Thomas Ball, Benjamin W. Bowman, Stephen N. Brown, Richard Emmons, Asmus Hill, Alanson T. Knox, John W. Lumley, Nathaniel Lightfoot, Jarvis McIntyre, Jacob Ostrum, Sam'l Oatcalt, Hanson Perkins, George W. Sawyer, Simeon W. Spencer, Edmon M. Slater, Rolin G. Story, George Vanderwacker, James P. Vickers, James Vincent, Martin Vandyke, Duane W. Weller, Cyrus L. Warren.

Deserted.

Corporal Henry L. Vanderwacker.
Privates Fred Labontes, Robt. Richmon, Wm. Reggolds.

LIST OF COMMISSIONED OFFICERS AND ENLISTED MEN,

Wounded while in the Service.

FIELD AND STAFF.

Col. Thos. W. Humphrey, severely wounded in foot, May 19, 1863, at Vicksburg, Miss.; killed in action at Guntown, Miss., June 10, 1864.

Lieut. Col. Wm. T. Avery, severely wounded in thighs, May, 1863, at Vicksburg, Miss.

Surgeon John W. Green, severely wounded in neck at siege of Spanish Fort, Ala.

Sergt. Maj. Charley Curtis, wounded slightly in back at siege of Spanish Fort, Ala.

COMPANY "A."

Corporal John Kennedy, wounded in left arm in skirmish at Lake Providence, La., Feb. 10, 1863; also in left knee at Nashville, Tenn., Dec. 15, 1864; leg amputated.

In charge on enemy's works at Vicksburg, Miss., May 19 and 22, 1863. *2nd Lieut.* Jas. E. Sponable, in right foot. *Corporals* Wm. H. Saunders, Geo. W. Sponable. *Privates* Robt. G. Smith, Dan'l W. Mitchell, Libbeus Olcott, John H. Beam, Augustus J. Fletcher, Theodore Ham, John H. Howard, Justus R. Henry, Andrew J. Jones, Wilford Mallory, Smith Nolan, Richard Pillion, Silas H. Roy, Nelson F. Shearer, Jas. G. Williams, Frank Shores. *Private* John Howard, wounded June 20, 1863, in back of head, by fragment of our shell, while on duty in rifle-pits as sharpshooter. *Private* Sam'l Snyder, leg broken by explosion at Fort De Russey, March 16, 1864.

At Blair's Plantation, La., April 12, 1864. *Sergt.* Benj. S. Parker, in left leg and side. *Corporal* Lafayette Wands. *Privates* Christopher Conley, John C. Cook, Coe Kilgore, Geo. W. Hamilton, Henry E. Knapp.

At Guntown, Miss., June 10, 1864. *Privates* Wilbur F. Morris, John Wallace, Jeremiah Dervine.

At Spanish Fort, Ala., March, 1864. *Sergt.* Wm. H. Saunders, in throat. *Privates* Smith Nolan, in knee;

ILLINOIS INFANTRY VOLUNTEERS. 233

Joseph Forney, in breast; Elijah Lyons, in foot; Henry Hilflicker, in ear; Dan'l W. Mitchell, in elbow; Geo. W. Hamilton, in hand; Wm. W. Hamilton, in side. *Corporals* Wm. H. Saunders, Lewis Grey, and *Privates* Parley Inman, Emery J. Ladd, wounded while with detachment in Georgia campaign.

COMPANY "B."

Private John Sexton, in skirmish near Lake Providence, La., Feb. 10, 1863.

At Vicksburg, Miss., May 19 and 22, 1863. *Sergeant* Chas. Anderson *Corporal* John Horan (died of wounds). *Privates* Benj. Easton (died of wounds), Thos. Moore, John Martin, Alfred M. Horton, David Cox, Alex. S. Cummings, Orlando Loper, James R. Manning, Wm. R. Stevenson, John Sexton, Job H. Westbury (died of wounds.) *Private* David F. Studley, wounded June 10, 1863, at Vicksburg, Miss., (died of wounds).

At Guntown, Miss., June 10, 1864. *Lieut.* Jas. M. Tisdel, severely, in leg. *Sergt.* Stephen A. Rollins (died of wounds.) *Corporal* Joseph Sweetapple. *Privates* Henry Williams (died of wounds), Washington Porter. *Private* John H. Searls, wounded in action near Baker's Ridge, Ga.

COMPANY "C."

In charge on enemy's works at Vicksburg, Miss., Jan. 19 and 22, 1863. *1st Lieut.* Otis H. Smith, in hand. *Sergts.* Wm. H. Stoddard, in thigh, (died of wounds); Samuel Cutter, in shoulder. *Corporals* Chas. Bigsby, in hand, knee and heel, (died of wounds); Edgar J. Dodge, in shoulder, (died of wounds). *Privates* Wm. H. Chilsen, in hand; John W. King, in hand; Patrick Hovey, in thigh; Reuben Cook, in hand, (died of wounds); Dan'l S. Broughton, in neck, (died of wounds); Wm. Brown, in body, (died of wounds); Alpheus Cook, in shoulder; Chas. Chilson, in hand; Theodore W. Goodsell, in hand; Wm. Marshall, in thigh; Ira M. Pierce, in thigh; Randolph E. Slawson, in head; Edwin E. Winney, in hand; Jas W. Smith, in head, (died of wounds). *Private* Robt. Buchanan, in arm, at battle of Yellow Bayou, La., May 18, 1864. *Sergt.* Geo. W. Reynolds, in arm, at Guntown, Miss., June 10, 1864.

Corporal Wm. Gerrett, in arm, at Guntown, Miss., June 10, 1864. *Private* Dan'l S. Cummings, in wrist, at siege of Spanish Fort, March 27, 1865. *Private* Wm. Marshall, in thigh, at Atlanta, Ga., (died of wounds).

COMPANY "D."

At Vicksburg, Miss., May 19 and 22, 1863. *Captain* Edward J. Cook (died of wounds June 11, 1863). *Sergt.* Chas. C. Barnes (died of wounds June 1, 1863). *Privates* Wm. B. Fry, J. Hutson, Andrew Olson, Henry C. Bywater, Chas. H. Francisco (died of wounds June 7, 1863), John Leggett, Mark Reble, (also wounded June 14, 1863), Henry M. Shannon, George Swindell, Levi Waterman. *Private* Henry Arndt, wounded June 4, 1863, while in camp, by shot from the enemy. *Private* Alonzo D. Crocker, accidentally shot in hand, May 20, 1863, (died of wounds.) *Private* James Wallis, in battle at Cane River, La., April 22, 1864.

At Guntown, Miss., June 10, 1864. *Captain* John E. Beckley. *Corporal* John H. Doran. *Privates* Wm. Diamond, John Keepsel, Thos. Powers, Wm. Mullen.

COMPANY "E."

Sergt. John Prowse, accidentally, in hand, by discharge of his own gun, Dec. 21, 1862. *Corporal* Thos. Cahill, in knee, at Lake Providence, La., Feb. 21, 1863.

At Vicksburg, Miss., May 19 and 22, 1863. *Sergts.* John W. Burnside; Frank M. Jewett, in thigh, by a piece of shell. *Corporal* James Stevenson, by shell. *Privates* Chas. Burton, in shoulder, by a ball; David Little, in hand; John Murphy, in hand; John Morse; George Kline, by explosion of a shell; Clark Everest, by a shell. *Private* Albert Wheelon, May 23, 1863, in hand, by a ball. *Corporal* Amos Capron, Jan. 14, 1863, in shoulder. *Sergt.* Clark Rogers, in thigh, Aug. 6, 1864, near Atlanta, Ga.

COMPANY "F."

At Vicksburg, Miss. *Privates* Peter Munis, in leg; Nicholas Myer, in side; Robt. Feely, in hand; Cyrus Wheelock, in hip; Wm. J. Dailey, in hand; G. W. French, in shoulder; H. Kerr; Joseph Cutforth, in foot and ancle,

ILLINOIS INFANTRY VOLUNTEERS. 235

(died of wounds); Henry Hess, Martin Tiffany. *Private* Peter Weitzel, in hand, April 12, 1864, at Blair's Plantation, La. *Corporal* Allen Giles, arm broken, March 16, 1864, at Fort De Russey.

At Guntown, Miss., June 10, 1864. *Capt.* Wm. H. Stewart, in thighs. *1st Lieut.* M. F. Ellsworth, in hand. *Private* Patrick McNeeny, in leg. *Private* Con. Lutzen, in foot, at Spanish Fort, Ala.

COMPANY "G."

At Vicksburg, Miss. *Sergts.* Charles W. Ives, in hips, severely, by minnie ball; Jeremiah Wilcox, in hand, slightly, by minnie ball; Daniel B. Cornell, in face, severely, by minnie ball; Dwight S. Gookins, in hand, slightly, by minnie ball. *Corporals* Henry L. Potter, in face, slightly, by minnie ball; Richard O. Gunn, in hand, severely, by minnie ball. *Privates* Peter Byron, in thigh, severely, by minnie ball; Jacob Seibert, in hand, slightly, by minnie ball; Benson R. Arbunckle, in back, slightly, by minnie ball; Robert Hannah, in ancle and thigh, slightly, by minnie ball; Albert Blood, in head, slightly, by buck shot; Eli Brainard, severely, in both shoulders, arm, neck and hand, by five minnie balls; Carrol J. Pray, in shoulder, severely, by minnie ball, (died of wounds.)

At Guntown, Miss., June 10, 1864. *Privates* Michael Hogan, in thigh, severely, (leg amputated, died of wounds); John Morrison, through body, severely, by minnie ball.

At Spanish Fort, Ala. *Privates* Jacob Seibert, in left arm, severely, by piece of shell, (arm amputated); George A. Oaks, in neck, slightly, by minnie ball; Peter Wiese, in leg, slightly, by piece of shell. *Corporal* Robt. Hannah, in breast and arm, near Atlanta, Ga. *Private* Henry F. Childs, in left arm, severely, by minnie ball, at Memphis, Tenn., (arm amputated.)

COMPANY "H."

At Vicksburg, Miss. *Capt.* James H. Wetmore, in thigh, severely, by minnie ball. *1st Lieut.* Wm. B. Walker, in back, by falling of limb of tree, shot off by shell. *Sergt.* Schuyler Marvin, thumb of right hand shot off. *Corporals* Moses Frazier, in shoulder, severely, by minnie ball;

Richard Bailey. *Privates* John Q. Adams, in right foot, by minnie ball; George W. Bellknapp, in right arm, in elbow, severely; George Clark, in right arm, by shell; Hartwell S. Mead, in left breast, severely, by buck shot and shell; Van Buren Truesdell, in right thigh, severely, by minnie ball; James Walsh, in arm, severely, by minnie ball.

At Guntown, Miss., June 10, 1864. *Privates* Gideon C. Hammer, in arm, severely; Jackson Hammer, in arm, slightly; Arthur A. Sheldon, right arm broken by minnie ball; James Welch, in right wrist, by minnie ball. *Private* Colen Hughes, wounded in right shoulder, near Big Black, May 17, 1863.

COMPANY "I."

At Vicksburg, Miss. *2nd Lieut.* Converse Pearce, in right arm. *Sergt.* Asa L. Weaver, left fore finger shot off. *Privates* Horace B. Allen, right fore finger shot off; James Kee, left fore finger shot off; Joseph C. Johnston, in left breast; Francis Corkins, right fore finger shot off; Edward P. Slater, right fore finger shot off; Patrick Crowley, in left side. George H. Burgess, June 26, 1863, in hand and wrist. Christopher Kalahan, June 20, 1863, through mouth and neck; H. P. Schuyler.

At Guntown, Miss., June, 10, 1864. *1st Lieut.* Thomas H. Jackson, in right arm, severely, (died of wounds). *Corporal* Charles W. Carpenter, in right arm. *Private* Samuel S. Crabtree, right arm broken by a piece of shell.

At Spanish Fort, Ala. *Sergt.* Asa L. Weaver, in shoulder, slightly. *Corporal* John W. Lockwood, in hand, slightly. *Privates* Patrick Crowley, in right arm, slightly; David Edward, in shoulder, slightly; Franklin E. Cox, in head, slightly.

COMPANY "K."

At Vicksburg, Miss. *Sergt.* John Vanantwerp, second finger of right hand shot off. *Corporals* Henry Morgan, tip of fore finger shot off; Joseph P. Smith, shot in back while planting colors on a hill in advance of regiment. *Privates* Cordenio Bruce, in right shoulder, slightly; George O. Ellsworth, in left side, slightly, by a piece of shell; Gideon B. Lewis, shot through right leg below the knee; Schuyler

Wakefield, in left leg by musket shot, (leg amputated); Jas. Dymond, fore finger of left hand shot off; Charles E. Sherman, fore finger of right hand shot off; Martin Butler, fore finger of right hand shot off; Wm. Hutchins, in right hand slightly; George Stockwell. James B. Scougall, May 24, 1863, left toe of left foot shot off by accident. Wm. Gibbs, severely wounded in knee, Aug. 12, 1864, near Atlanta, Ga. Stephen Rodawalt, in hand, slightly, at Spanish Fort, Ala.

LIST OF COMMISSIONED OFFICERS AND ENLISTED MEN KILLED IN ACTION.

Colonel Thomas W. Humphrey, at Guntown, Miss., June 10, 1864.

COMPANY "A."

Privates Frank Shoris, and James F. Smith, killed at Vicksburg, Miss., May 22, 1863; Samuel Snyder, killed at Fort De Russey by explosion of shell, March 16, 1864; Wm. F. Wallace, killed at siege of Spanish Fort, Ala., March 28, 1865; Michael P. O'Neil, killed in action at Guntown, Miss., June 10, 1864.

COMPANY "B."

Sergt. Stephen A. Rollins, and *Private* Henry Williams, killed at Guntown, Miss., June 10, 1864. *Private* Job Westbury, killed at Vicksburg, Miss., May 22, 1863.

COMPANY "C."

Capt. Jason B. Manzer, killed at Vicksburg, Miss., May 22, 1863. *Privates* Levi Harp, killed at Vicksburg, Miss., May 19, 1863; Thomas J. Brown, killed by the enemy while on transport on the Red River Expedition, April 12, 1864; John De Groat, killed at Vicksburg, Miss., May 22, 1863; Lewis Deno, killed at Vicksburg, May 19, 1863; John M. Hunt, missing, and supposed killed at Vicksburg, May 22, 1863; Samuel H. Jackson, killed by explosion of caisson at Fort De Russey, Ark., March 17, 1864; Wm. Marshall, killed near Atlanta, Ga., July 23, 1864; Marion Pease, killed at Vicksburg, Miss., May 22, 1863; William

Shutts, missing in action, and supposed killed at Vicksburg, Miss., May 22, 1863.

COMPANY "D."

Corporals Thomas McLean, and Enos H. Barnes, killed at Vicksburg, Miss., May 22, 1863. *Privates* Andrew Hoff, and Carl Selm, missing in action, and supposed killed at Vicksburg, Miss., May 22, 1863; Wm. R. Miller, killed at Vicksburg, May 19, 1863; Paul Shawl, and Elijah P. Weaver, killed at Guntown, Miss., June 10, 1864.

COMPANY "E."

Privates Wm. Bassett and James Kennedy, killed at Vicksburg, Miss., May 19, 1863; Elisha W. Higley and Geo. Reimon, missing, and supposed killed, and Henry Maddick, killed, at Vicksburg, Miss., May 22, 1863.

COMPANY "F."

Sergt. James Tibbitts, killed at Vicksburg, Miss., May 22, 1863. *Corporal* Oliver E. Pomeroy, killed at Vicksburg, Miss., May 22, 1863. *Privates* Wm. A. Churchill, killed at Guntown, Miss., June 10, 1864; Patrick Kelley, killed at Vicksburg, Miss, May 22, 1863; Daniel W. Ryan, killed at Vicksburg, Miss., May 19, 1863.

COMPANY "G."

Capt. Elliott N. Bush, killed at Guntown, Miss., June 10, 1864. *Privates* John E. Benedict, killed at Vicksburg, Miss., May 19, 1863; Wm. E. Gunn, killed at Vicksburg, Miss., May 22, 1863.

COMPANY "H."

Corporal Richard D. Bailey, killed at Guntown, Miss., June 10, 1864. *Privates* Julius Buttke, and Willard Kimball, killed at Guntown, Miss., June 10, 1864; Thomas R. Mead, killed at Vicksburg, Miss., May 19, 1863.

COMPANY "I."

Corporal Samuel E. Thomas, killed at Guntown, Miss., June 10, 1864. *Privates* Conrad Goltman, and David F. Huntley, killed at Vicksburg, Miss., May 22, 1863.

COMPANY "K."

Capt. Gabriel Cornwell, killed at Vicksburg, Miss., May 22, 1863. *Corporal* Joseph P. Smith, killed at Vicksburg, Miss., May 22, 1863. *Privates* Wm. F. Baker, and Gabriel J. Cornwell, killed at Vicksburg, Miss., May 22, 1863; Anson Perkins, killed at Clouterville, La., April 24, 1864.

LIST OF CAMPAIGNS AND BATTLES IN WHICH THE REGIMENT TOOK PART.

General Grant's Campaign in Northern Mississippi; Tallahatchie river.

Campaign against Vicksburg; Grand Gulf, Raymond, Champion Hills; charges on works at Vicksburg, May 19 and 22, 1863; siege. Operations at and around Natchez, Miss., during Summer and Fall of 1863.

Red River expedition; Fort De Russey, Old river, Clouterville, Mansouri, Yellow Bayou. Guntown, June 10, 1864.

Campaign against Price, in Arkansas and Missouri, in the Fall of 1864.

Campaign against Hood in Tennessee; Nashville, December 15 and 16, 1864.

Campaign against Mobile, Ala. Siege of Spanish Fort. Charge on works, April 8, 1865. Fort Blakely, April 9, 1865.

Battles in which the Detachment of the Regiment participated during General Sherman's Georgia Campaign: Kenesaw Mountain, Chattahoochee River, Atlanta, Ezra Church, Jonesboro, Lovejoy Station.

Distance traveled by the Regiment while in the service— 9,960 miles.

TABULAR STATEMENT, SHOWING NUMBER OF COMMISSIONED OFFICERS AND ENLISTED MEN MUSTERED OUT, TRANSFERRED, DISCHARGED, DIED, DESERTED, AND AGGREGATE NUMBER BELONGING TO THE REGIMENT DURING THE SERVICE.

	No. to muster out.				Whole No. enlisted men transferred.		Enlisted men discharged in service.			Deaths.			Desertions.		Aggregate No. of officers and enlisted men ever in the Reg't.
	Commissioned Officers.	Original enlisted men.	Recruits, enlisted men.	Officers resigned and promoted.	Prior to muster out of Regiment, recruits left at Montgomery.	Prior to muster out, to Invalid Corps, etc.	For disability.	For promotion to other Regiments.	For other causes.	Com. Officers. In battle and from wounds received in action.	Enlisted men.	From Disease.	Enlisted men.	Enlisted men of African descent.	
Field and Staff	9	6		5			1	3	2	1		1			12*
Company "A,"	3	51	10	1	22	10	15	3	4		11	12	3		146
" "B,"	3	49	11	4	14	3	17	3			6	17	2	1	129
" "C,"	3	47	20	1	19	3	13			1	17	21	2	3	150
" "D,"	3	33	17		17	3	21	8	6		12	12	3		129
" "E,"	3	47	21		24	4	22	2		1	6	19	2		153
" "F,"	2	42	7	2	7		13	2			7	20	5	1	113
" "G,"	3	54	7	3	9	6	8		6	1	4	24	2		128
" "H,"	3	43	8	1	18	2	22	5	6		5	15	4	2	131
" "I,"	3	42	12	1	15	7	24	5		1	5	12	4		130
" "K,"	3	41	7	1	17	6	27	5		1	5	24	4		134
Total......	29	449	115	15	162	47	182	26	22	4	78	176	31	7	1343

* This aggregate includes merely those belonging to F. and S. at the organization of Regiment, and those subsequently appointed from civil life; all others are accounted for in the Companies as "promoted" or "transferred."

www.ingramcontent.com/pod-product-compliance
Lightning Source LLC
Chambersburg PA
CBHW031745230426
43669CB00007B/491